# LOCO WEED—
# THE MARIJUANA PRIMER

*Nick Columbini*

America Star Books

First printing

America Star Books has allowed this work to remain exactly as the author intended, verbatim, without editorial input.

Softcover 9781611027235
PUBLISHED BY AMERICA STAR BOOKS, LLLP
www.americastarbooks.com

Printed in the United States of America

*In the Beginning...*

And the Lord said to Adam and Eve, "You are My finest creations, and I am proud of you. Thus, I give to you all Paradise, and give you mastery over all animals, and call you my children."

The Lord said, "All this is yours, but one—you are to restrain from eating of the Tree in the center of the garden, neither shall you touch it for it is poisonous and forbidden fruit."

And Adam and Eve were happy and lived in glory.

One day, though, a serpent approached and said unto Eve, "Eat of that Tree. It is the tree of knowledge…the tree of revelation. Eat of that tree and your minds shall be opened and you shall be like gods."

And Eve knew but it was wrong. But Eve trusted unto the serpent and disobeyed the Lord, and ate of the Cannabis Tree. And then Eve told Adam that it wasn't toxic and that it was an innocuous, benign, natural substance, and that he, too, should eat. And, thus, Adam succumbed to the first documented case of peer pressure and ate of the Cannabis flowers and buds.

Immediately Eve's eyes were opened and she said "I am naked." And immediately Adam's eyes opened and he said, "I am ashamed." This was not the tree of knowledge. It was not the tree of life. It was not the tree of good. It was the tree of ego…the tree of pride…the tree of good and evil mixed…of good contaminated of evil.

And the Cannabis Tree delivered man into false pride and self-indulgence and self-centric idolatry and narcissism, which quickly rose to excessive heights.

And thus, Adam and Eve had committed the original sin and were poisoned and became severe, and never again found true harmony and balance in nature or in life.

Paradise Lost.

# LOCO WEED: DISCLAIMER

Loco Weed is a street term for marijuana. Technically cannabis (marijuana) is a species of the *Cannabaceae* family of plants, and not one of the several plants of the genera *Oxytropis* or *Astragalus* more commonly known as loco weed. It is, however, a powerful psychoactive substance that does cause an intoxication that in many ways mimics some of the "craziness" and "bizarre behavior" seen with Astragalus use by animals (intoxication, depression, lethargy, eyes dull and staring, accidents, withdrawal from other animals, abortions and birth defects, possible violence if stressed, and neurological damage with long term use.) In this sense, the term loco weed for marijuana is apropos.

This book makes no pretense about the subject matter.

This book does not intend to present the pros and cons of marijuana use. It is not intended to convey any discussion, whatsoever, about any "benefits" of marijuana. It is solely intended to describe the negative consequences of marijuana use and abuse as experienced by millions of users over these past 50 years. Marijuana has killed people. It has crippled many more. It has destroyed the quality of life for, yet, many more. It has destroyed relationships and families. It is not the benign, innocuous, natural "herb" substance that some people make it out to be.

While there is a strong and growing base of pro-marijuana enthusiasts across the United States, and while there is a corresponding substantial influence by users, academicians, lobbyists and public policy lawmakers—the fact remains that marijuana is a danger to self and society and this needs to be reiterated again and again. For this, the author makes no apology.

America is dying. Drugs are one of the greatest reasons. Marijuana is the most widely used of all the illegal drugs. Therefore, even if only ten percent of the population of users experience negative consequences from marijuana use (and the percentage is much more), it results in millions of people who suffer health consequences, mental illness, family dysfunction, accidents, or chemical dependency.

This goal of this author is to support the health, safety and welfare of our youth and families. Toward this end, this book exposes the real dimension of marijuana and strips away the spurious claims of the pro-marijuana industry.

It certainly is not the intent of this author to offend anyone because of differences of opinions. If a reader is inadvertently offended this author does apologize.

Finally, this author has reviewed hundreds of articles and studies, and has spoken to many former users and addicts, and as such, it is the intent to present these series of findings in a concise and understandable manner. Toward this end the reader may find one or two concepts he/she disagrees with or where newer research disproves a previous finding. But even if a specific finding is no longer current, this does not invalidate this book. If the reader disputes even ten percent of these findings it does not invalidate the entire premise of this book, i.e., the other ninety percent of the book is accurate and valid in presentation, content and interpretation.

# Table of Contents

# OPERATIONAL PREMISE

*"I have reviewed—literally—hundreds of articles and studies on marijuana. I have never seen one study that even hints that marijuana is a protective factor for positive youth development. I have never seen one study that states that marijuana use supports healthy families. I have never seen one study that concludes that marijuana use builds strong communities. I have never seen one study that has proven that marijuana is a safe drug. In fact, overwhelmingly, the findings are exactly the opposite for all four cases."*

—Nick Columbini

For the reader's personal edification this book then begins with this sentence: "Marijuana is a powerful, toxic, and mind-altering addictive psychoactive drug."

Marijuana is not an innocuous, benign drug. The myth that marijuana is a harmless recreational drug has been disproved through hundreds of scientific studies and countless hours of research. Marijuana is wrought with real and significant adverse side effects, such that no one can ever guarantee the safety of marijuana use.

Furthermore, any person with a high value on the health, safety and welfare of America's children and families should never recommend the use of marijuana for recreational purposes. Of the hundreds of studies for youth development and for enhancing healthy families, no study ever recommended marijuana use as a positive factor for human growth and development.

Here then, lies one of the greatest dangers of marijuana: *it is underestimated as a powerful pharmacologic, mind altering substance.* In this regard marijuana is not fully appreciated for what it really is—people do not give it serious consideration. Society disregards the inherent dangers, and before they know it at least 10-to-25 percent of users (up to 75 percent of teens) experience grave—even catastrophic consequences.

In one study by the National Household Survey on Drug Abuse (NHSDA), it was reported that among those using marijuana on 12 or more days during the past year, 58 percent of people had one problem that they related to their marijuana use, 41 percent had two problems and 28 percent had at least three problems that they related to their marijuana use.

The problems associated with marijuana use were greatest among the youngest age groups. Nearly 75 percent of children and teens (12-to-17 year-olds) who used marijuana on 12 or more days in the past year experienced significant problems related to use, and 42 percent experienced three or more problems, including loss of control over their use.

Marijuana is a drug. Marijuana is toxic. Marijuana is a powerful psycho-active substance. Marijuana is addictive. Marijuana is a gateway drug. Marijuana has adverse physical effects. Marijuana has adverse mental effects. Marijuana has adverse emotional effects. Marijuana has adverse spiritual effects. Marijuana has adverse social and relationship effects. Marijuana is dangerous. Marijuana can and has destroyed the quality of life for millions of people. Most certainly, marijuana has legitimately earned its reputation as a dangerous drug.

Youth and families alike need to take heed. Marijuana is like dynamite, and one can never predict when it will explode. Too many have found out too late, that marijuana is a weapon of mass destruction.

# AN OPEN MESSAGE FOR PARENTS

Over the past few years society has been inundated with a whole new level of half-truths and misconceptions about marijuana. The result is that after a generation of awareness of the dangers of marijuana use resulting in a significant decrease in use, youth and parents both are being misinformed and are now adopting a more tolerant stance such as "At least it is not hard drugs." The outcome was predictable: marijuana use is now spreading and progressing to epidemic proportions.

The fact is that nothing has changed about marijuana over these years, except that it is more potent and more powerful than ever, and if anything is now more dangerous. Marijuana was and remains a powerful, addictive, and potentially toxic, mind-altering drug. There has never yet, been a study showing that marijuana use is beneficial for youth development. In fact, virtually every study demonstrates exactly the opposite.

Parents have an obligation to continue to protect their children from marijuana use. The results of even "casual" use can be devastating to the youth and family. Yes, many teens go through a period of rebellion, but the changes among marijuana users have a whole different flavor including anger and displaced rage, isolation, decreased interest in academics or sports, problematic behaviors, secretiveness, disrespect, association with questionable peers, mental or emotional lability, distorted perceptions, difficulty in thinking and problem solving, increase in anxiety and perhaps paranoia, a growing need to use it "to relax", and even depression and possibly suicidal ideation.

Marijuana is not just a drug, but a mind-altering drug, i.e., one that has special immediate and long lasting effects on the brain. It alters moods, changes sensory perception, alters one's stream of consciousness, disrupts normal cognitive functions, and enhances or intensifies sense modalities including skin pain and pressure receptors, autonomic functions, and comfort and discomfort stimuli. It alters ones perception of time. It alters functional association. And there is an alteration in one's state and manner of awareness. It narrows the amount of diverse contents in the focus of attention, leading to a type of absorption in an object or event to the exclusion of everything else—a type of tunnel vision with a corresponding reduction in the peripheral vision. The result here is that a marijuana user may not be able to effectively function in a manner consistent with multi-tasking. The effect on memory is mixed, but there is evidence to support impairment of short term memory, i.e., that short term memory is shorter and that this effect may be persistent but not permanent. Long term memory may also be impaired as well, but where marijuana users may better remember the emotion expressed during an event rather than the detail itself when under the influence.

One study published in the Journal of Neuroscience said that with even occasional or casual marijuana smokers, the amygdala and nucleus accumbens regions of the brains were abnormally shaped, and the nucleus accumbens was larger. The more a person used marijuana, the more pronounced the brain changes. Even low-level marijuana use may make a person more vulnerable to addiction, or to changing their emotions or thought processes, according to the researchers.

Another study in the journal National Proceedings of the Academy of Sciences, stated that teens who smoke marijuana see their IQs drop as adults, and deficits persist even after quitting according to a new study. The findings are consistent with speculation that cannabis use in adolescence when the brain is undergoing critical development, may have neurotoxic effects according to the researchers, and the average I.Q. point drop for the smokers was 8 points.

A study released in the New England Journal of Medicine, authored by scientists from the National Institute of Drug Abuse linked marijuana to several adverse health effects. The review shows that addiction increases both for young users as well as for daily users. The scientists focused on marijuana's harmful effects on teens, and found a number of adverse health effects leading the scientists to a medium-to-high level of confidence for marijuana users to develop addiction or addiction to marijuana and other substances, for abnormal brain development, for marijuana users to progress onto other drugs, for users to develop depression or anxiety, for developing symptoms of chronic bronchitis, for increased motor vehicle accidents, and they found a high level of confidence for diminished lifetime achievement.

Certainly more than one parent has reported that their children had personality changes after beginning marijuana use.

This book presents a technical explanation for the dangers of marijuana use. It applies to all, but especially to youth. Parents need to know the basics, and need to present them in a firm, no-nonsense and disapproving manner to their youth. Lives depend upon it.

Parents, by all means continue to show love and kindness, but also firmness to your children. Take a strong disapproval of use stance regarding marijuana, and find out the facts to share with your children so they understand the harm that does result from marijuana. One of the reasons teens do not realize the dangers of marijuana is because they do not readily see the damaging physical effects. But unlike tobacco or alcohol, the real damage from marijuana is not necessarily the physical harm to the body, but rather the negative mental effects on the brain, the emotional changes interfering with the stages of development, and the social changes interfering with relationship building and bonding with family and friends. These changes are usually not recognized as readily as physical effects, but are every bit as real and as damaging over several years. Of course, the potential for marijuana addiction with the resultant symptoms of buildup of tolerance, increase in use, increase in desire to use, mood swings when not using, and loss of control (inability to cut down or quit when one recognizes there is a problem), are all hallmark signs of marijuana dependence.

Remember, too, that research shows that building certain Protective Factors can reduce the likelihood of your children using or abusing alcohol, tobacco or other drugs. So a few tips for raising drug-free children, include:

—Spend quality and quantity time with your children! For children, being loved, valued and accepted by means of praising, encouragement and affection are key determinants in healthy, non-risk behavior. Research shows that the more support the better.

—Raise your children with belief in God, and practice your family faith in a church, synagogue, or mosque. The family practice of religion is a strong predictor of health and development.

—Give sound parental supervision, especially after school, nights and weekends. Monitoring your children's whereabouts and what they are doing may be the most important indicator of healthy behavior. Don't leave children alone to raise themselves.

—Become involved in your children's activities! Children are proud when their parents are involved in a meaningful way.

—Be a positive role model. For example, if you smoke or drink at home or gamble in a casino you invite your children to start those very behaviors, and often they start earlier than you did. Research also shows a relationship between a family's history of alcoholism or drug use, and the higher probability of your own children developing those very problems. Be a positive role model. Children naturally copy parent's words and behaviors.

—Guide your children to respect opinions of parents and adults over those of their peers in regard to important decision making. Respect is a key determinant of positive youth development.

—Help your children develop high aspirations for school and education. Help them with homework (at least one hour each day), help them to care about their school, help them read for pleasure at least three hours per week, help them understand the need for work beginning with chores at home, and help them to become motivated to do well both in school, sports and other activities of interest.

—Most importantly, teach your children family values like family traditions, caring, honesty, responsibility, restraint, respect, kindness, charity, and the work ethic.

There are no guarantees, but parents who are aware of their own drinking or drug behaviors, who give support, who show their disapproval around alcohol or drug use, and who monitor their children are significantly more likely to have children who are less involved in drinking, substance abuse or problematic behavior. Remember, discipline is not about punishment. Discipline is about sharing in a way of life that is healthy and wholesome, predictable, mutually supportive, and one which helps to reach family-shared goals.

# REALITY CHECK

*Which answer is the MOST Correct?*

Research has proven that Marijuana can be a causative factor for:

1) Schizophrenia
2) In lowering a person's I. Q.
3) Panic Attacks
4) Psychosis
5) Chronic Lung Disease
6) Cancer
7) Impotency
8) Amotivational Syndrome
9) Depression
10) Delusions of persecution
11) Hallucinations
12) Accidents
13) Lower Life Satisfaction
14) Cognitive Impairment
15) Mood Fluctuations & Emotional Lability
16) Suicide
17) Miscarriage and Birth Defects
18) Dependency and Addiction
19) Lower "Global Life Functioning"
20) Family Dysfunction
21) Testicular Shrinkage.
22) Gynecomastia
23) Insomnia and Sleep disorders
24) Withdrawal Syndrome
25) *All* of the Above

# THE CONFUSION

There is a very special case when it comes to discussion about drug abuse and drugs as weapons of mass destruction in America today and that case is cannabis, more commonly known as marijuana. In this regard and especially because marijuana use has been a drug of choice for youth and young adults, it is important to highlight this as a special case with special circumstances.

There are six distinct reasons that marijuana is so poorly understood:

First, marijuana seems to lack the immediate negative consequences that other drugs have such as toxic properties whereby one can die from overdose, or where people can experience a rapid onset of physical addiction. Marijuana has more subtle long term effects that are not as easily recognizable as with the other so-called "harder" drugs. This does not mean that cannabis is a harmless, benign substance, but because of this property people often falsely conclude that *"marijuana is not dangerous."*

Second, the research which has been available historically was poor, often quotes old findings, is misinterpreted, is based upon studies utilizing the lower marijuana THC content of the 60's and 70's, or it presents results too specific to be generalized to the real population. A review of the studies also reveals that the marijuana research often has biases or otherwise spurious interpretation that affects validity, reliability or generalizability.

Third, people tend to compare marijuana against the other drugs, giving them a false sense of security, for example, "Well it isn't as dangerous as alcohol." This is fallacious reasoning, a common type of defect in a logic model. From a logic model, such a comparison is invalid as it is irrelevant to the point. For instance, this model would imply that because arsenic does not kill as many people as cyanide, strychnine or mercury, it must therefore be "safer." In this way, marijuana somehow has actually gained a positive value among youth because it (falsely) seems not as dangerous as the other drugs.

Fourth, there is a general tendency by marijuana enthusiasts and users to refuse to believe the true and accurate research based upon their belief that "the research is biased due to governmental funding," or is otherwise falsified. So when science demonstrates a withdrawal syndrome with cannabis thereby demonstrating an actual marijuana addiction, it is disregarded or totally ignored by the majority of marijuana users and pro-marijuana advocates.

The fact is that our treatment agencies are full of marijuana dependent individuals with personal testimonials to the power and dangers of marijuana, but these people, too, are similarly dismissed as irrelevant converts (even though they were themselves part of that pro-marijuana establishment at one time.) In fact, according to the Treatment Episode Data Survey, of the two million people admitted into treatment clinics each year, 18 percent (and as high as 24 percent has been reported) of those patients say that marijuana is their *primary* drug of addiction, and tens of thousands more have dual-diagnosis with another drug and marijuana (most usually alcohol.)

It is not just anecdotal stories that give us clues to the true dangers of marijuana use. Today, both research and science have demonstrated beyond a shadow of a doubt that marijuana, like any other pharmacological substance, is a powerful drug with far reaching short term and long term consequences. In fact, due to the nature of marijuana as a psycho-active, mood altering substance, the implications for long term dysfunction and/or disorder is even more pronounced.

The fifth reason underlying the confusion is because of a richly funded pro-marijuana advocacy and lobbyist industry. The pro-marijuana industry is seriously intent on reversing all laws regarding the prohibition of the growing, cultivating, manufacturing, distribution, and use of marijuana. The industry is as strong as the alcohol industry, tobacco industry or gun/arms industry, and is well funded and well staffed. It has been said that the marijuana lobbying arm is now a 40-50 million dollar per year lobby. They employ tactics which undermine traditional non-use messages, and have now ventured into highly sophisticated marketing and advertising techniques which further erode confidence in the government's stance against the use of marijuana. In fact at this writing there is a lawsuit pending in Colorado to allow marijuana ads to be published in teen publications (currently the rules allow recreational marijuana businesses to advertise only in publications that are adult-oriented, i.e., no more than 30 percent of the publication's readership is reasonably expected to be under the age of 21.) The lawsuit argues the rules, which also restrict television, radio and outdoor advertising, are an unconstitutional restriction of free speech. Thus, the lawyers are involved to again exploit and widen the laws and promote marijuana use even to youth.

With the current findings of new monies that can be realized in the private sector—estimated to be a five billion dollar market for marijuana (nine billion by 2020), there is even more finding that people are switching stance—including one-time conservative businessmen as they see the profits that can be made through, yet, another drug. In the western states which have first legalized medical marijuana and more recently recreational marijuana, it is known as the "Green Rush"—the west experienced a gold rush, then a silver rush, and now because of all the money to be made—a "Marijuana Rush."

Finally, the most significant and influential source of the confusion is also the most obvious: the media. The hype, propaganda, marketing, debates, publications, television shows, movies, magazines, YouTube videos, blogs, social media postings, comedians, etc., all create an artificial set of opinions about marijuana based in half-truths and sound bites that are controversial and which undermine the science and research behind the findings.

Media has always publicly stated that it does not influence society but merely reflects upon it. But realistically everyone admits to the immense power of the press and the power of mass communication, the fact that the pen is mightier than the sword. People still speak of the classic example of the televised debate between Richard Nixon and John F. Kennedy, and how television led to Kennedy's triumph as the 35th president of the United States. This is why politicians strive to build the largest "war chest," to be able to buy the most media for their campaigns simply to influence voters. This is why industry will pay $3 million for a 30 second commercial during the Superbowl. Media shapes norms and changes culture. Media is economic power. Media is political power. Media is social power. Media has toppled governments. And media has refined, shaped and propelled the pro-marijuana argument into a finely honed production which tempts, encourages and confuses youth and adults everywhere.

Together, at the very least these six factors are causing a "role-confusion" for America—an identity crisis which at the very least is a growing apathy and disregard for the consequences of marijuana use and for the millions who suffer those consequences.

Who does support drug legalization? Is it the average American Family? Is it the experts who work with alcoholics and addicts every day trying to save the wasted lives and tragedies of drug use? Is it the nurses or physicians who find drug users in the hospital emergency rooms tens-of-thousands of times each year? Is it the law enforcement agencies that deal with the results of the marijuana user? No.

In general, the groups that constantly call for drug legalization are the marijuana-enthusiasts (users), marijuana lawyers and lobbyists, university professors who too often are operating from a theoretical but non-realistic model, liberals and civil liberties individuals looking to change government (this often includes people who would legalize everything for the highest goal "in the name of personal freedom",) artists and musicians looking to "find themselves" through self-expression, drug users, and, drug dealers (although drug dealers actually know that once corporate America assumes this—they are back on the street poor and without any job skills.)

In general, give neither give credence nor credibility to these groups. They have an ulterior motive, and that is only to legalize drugs…and many want to legalize all drugs and just use marijuana legalization as the first stepping stone in the process. They will use any and all propaganda, including the misinterpretation of facts to justify their position. In fact, one liberal foundation openly admitted that if someone defines even one useful benefit of marijuana, the foundation would continue funding the pro-marijuana activism. Thus, there is now the advent of "medical" marijuana.

There are also a number of "half-truths" about marijuana, exaggerations posed as "facts" spuriously presented to try to justify legalization. As one thinks them through very carefully, one finds they are myths and fallacies built upon faulty logic and do not stand when confronted with facts and experience.

1) *The European experience with marijuana legalization has not been disruptive*. This is false. The relaxing of drug laws and/or drug legalization in Europe has indeed been disruptive to the point that many social and human interest groups in Northern Europe have called for a return to the previous level of drug interdiction policies. In fact, the Netherlands is now a major producer and leading distributor of cannabis, heroin, cocaine, amphetamines and other synthetic drugs, and remains a medium consumer of illicit drugs. It has also been reported that serious crimes remain drug related, and also the number of "soft" drug cases is rising and currently accounts for 69% of criminal investigations
2) *Marijuana has never killed anyone*. One of the most popular beliefs of the marijuana enthusiasts is that marijuana never killed anyone. This is wrong. While there are few cases of human "acute toxicity to the point of death" by marijuana overdose, the fact is that as a drug marijuana has destroyed many lives—both in death, and more so, in chronic deterioration of the quality of life and in years of potential life lost. In fact in one major study, those treated

for addiction to cannabis had a higher mortality rate than controls (3.85 times higher), and higher if compared to the death rate risk of cocaine use disorder (2.96), or alcohol use disorder (3.83.)

3) *Marijuana isn't as bad as alcohol or tobacco…and they are legal.* The form of this statement is misleading. It should read, "Why legalize, yet, another drug?" They are all poisons, albeit, in different ways. Which is worse: arsenic, strychnine, or cyanide? They are all dangerous, they just have different pharmacological mechanisms and actions. Marijuana also has toxic properties dependent upon set and setting, quantity and frequency, potency, quality and purity, synergistic effects with other substances, threshold levels, tolerance, genetic susceptibility, physical maturation levels, personality stage of development, brain chemistry, previous experience of use, mental health status, status of social relationships, quality of life functioning, and other side effects associated with the hundreds of chemicals in a marijuana cigarette. Independent of the status of alcohol or nicotine, marijuana as a stand-alone is a dangerous drug that warrants continued prohibition of use.
4) *Marijuana has medicinal value.* Marijuana components or constituents may have some medicinal use for specific conditions, but if so they should be explored and developed for those traits with legitimate pharmacological research under the auspice of the Food and Drug Administration (F.D.A.) and not by legislative or political action. It is true that opium gave us important medicines such as morphine and codeine, but they were developed under the F.D.A. and opium itself is not legal in any raw form, nor should it be made so by wavering politicians or popular opinion.

5) *The drug laws are too "punitive."* In truth, the vast majority of those incarcerated are there because of the numerous offenses committed related to drug use, rather than for simple possession of marijuana. Imprisonment does include more serious drug offenses such as sale or distribution of drugs, but more so includes drug related stealing or burglary, or violent offenses including weapons possession. One analyst reported that 80 percent of all crime is drug related (i.e., crimes other than "simple possession") including marijuana. Indeed, the punishment should fit the crime, but this is not justification for the legalization of drugs.
6) *The research does not support all the government "propaganda" about the dangers of marijuana.* Again, this is false. Pro-marijuana enthusiasts are quick to dismiss government sponsored studies, but especially over these recent years hundreds of articles and studies—including biochemical and neurological findings—demonstrate more evidence than ever about the negative effects and consequences of marijuana use, abuse and dependency. Marijuana is, and remains, a powerful, toxic and addictive psychoactive drug.

This intent of this book is to explore these issues in more detail, to expose the myths, and to substantiate the truth about marijuana.

THE MYTH:

Marijuana is a Harmless Substance.

THE FACT:

*"More than 455,000 patients entered hospital emergency rooms with marijuana in their system in 2011, a 19% increase from just two years earlier."*

*—DAWN (Drug Abuse Warning Network.)*

# MARIJUANA...AN EXPOSÉ A DANGER TO HEALTH AND SAFETY!

*Why in the world would government ever legalize a third addictive drug?*

The sole purpose of this book is to expose the many myths and fallacies of the marijuana hype and propaganda, and to present the research that supports the notion that marijuana is a drug, is a powerful drug, and has numerous pharmacological properties many of which are dangerous, harmful and addictive in nature.

The cumulative impact of the research presented in this book should astonish the average reader. The research and argument(s) presented paint a holistic picture showing that there are significant health related reasons to avoid marijuana use as it is spreading throughout society. There is a plethora of dangers which have been identified, and there are dangers which society will yet experience.

There is an elephant in America's living room. It is real. It is significant. It is not going away. It causes more pain and hardship and destroys more people and families than most people will ever know. It is America's dirty little secret...

marijuana…"a harmless, social drug." Yet, nothing could be further from the truth,

The lack of understanding by Americans is not unique to marijuana. History is full of examples of mistakes that research has made over the years in pharmacologia, pharmacokinetics, and psychopharmacology (the branch of pharmacology dealing with the psychological effects of drugs.). One problem is that research, itself, is often incomplete or inconclusive when it comes to drugs.

Research has been critically wrong in many instances. For over one hundred years many said "elixir" or "tonic" (alcohol based potions) had remarkable healing powers, but eventually these salesmen became known as "snake oil salesmen" and they were exposed for their swindles and scams.

For years researchers thought cocaine to be a "miracle drug" that could lift one out of clinical depression, until it was found that cocaine heightened the very depression it was used to treat—even to suicidal levels.

Researchers through the 60s and 70s, said that no one could die from a heroin overdose (Consumer Union Report). When police and emergency rooms pointed to all the heroin deaths, researchers insisted that it was not the heroin causing the deaths but some ambiguous non-related dynamic they termed "Syndrome X."

One major study concluded that alcoholics could drink safely again (RAND Report), and before that study was disproved it did considerable damage to many thousands of recovering alcoholics who attempted again to return to social drinking.

In the early 1900s barbiturates, sedative-hypnotics and other tranquilizers were all said to be non-addictive. This was disproved in the 1950s when behavioral disturbances and the physical dependence of barbiturates became widely recognized. Many women in particular suffered from the over-prescription and use of these "non-addictive" substances.

In the 1960s pharmaceutical companies said that one could not become addicted to a new class of drugs—the benzodiazepines. They were wrong.

Health experts said that pregnant women could drink alcohol (they did not understand Fetal Alcohol Spectrum Disorder.)

Pharmaceutical companies said that the newer class of major tranquilizers and neuroleptics were not addictive—and many were.

Medicine tried cocaine based remedies and heroin based remedies and eventually found them inappropriate. Medicine is now seeing high rates of addiction and death from the newer classes of synthesized narcotic analgesics for pain management such as oxycodone and hydrocodone.

Of course, scores of drugs used for general treatment purposes have later been found to present not just side effects, but significant iatrogenic effects.

This, then brings us to marijuana. Without doubt, the main theme with marijuana is that everyone should be totally opposed to the use of marijuana as a recreational drug. Research on the health and safety effects of marijuana strongly correlates with many mental, emotional, psychological, physical and spiritual problems. In addition, many crimes, accidents, job and school performance problems have been associated with the use of marijuana. While not everyone that uses marijuana becomes drug dependent the reality is that as with alcohol and other drugs, marijuana use certainly can lead to profound, chronic and progressive chemical dependency.

Its use can be very serious, dangerous, and have a profound impact upon the quality of life for hundreds of thousands of Americans and their families. Marijuana can and does destroy lives. Similar to the height of use in the 1970s, marijuana use is again reaching epidemic proportions. It is a weapon of mass destruction.

Marijuana is the most commonly used illicit drug in the United States. A dry, shredded green/brown mix of flowers, stems, seeds, and leaves of the hemp plant cannabis sativa, cannabis indica, or cannabis ruderalis are cultivated every day. At one point there were 635 different strains found, with different attributes and effects. Cannabis Sativa is the primary plant for the drug use. It usually is smoked as a cigarette (joint), or in a pipe (bong), in a waterpipe, or in a vaporizer or vaped. It also is smoked in blunts, which are cigars that have been emptied of tobacco and refilled with marijuana, often in combination with another drug. Use also might include mixing marijuana in food or brewing it as a tea, or using it in cooking or other food products. These are known as edibles, or Marijuana Infused Products (MIPs.) As a more concentrated, resinous form it is called "hashish" and, as a sticky black liquid, "hash oil." The newest products are high concentrated THC "wax."

Marijuana smoke has a pungent and distinctive, usually sweet-and-sour odor. There are countless street terms for marijuana including pot, herb, weed, grass, widow, ganja, and hash, as well as terms derived from trademarked varieties of cannabis, such as, Northern Lights, Fruity Juice, Afghani #1, and a number of Skunk varieties. Of course it is also known as Loco Weed.

The main active chemical in marijuana is THC (delta-9-tetrahydrocannabinol). The membranes of certain nerve cells in the brain contain protein receptors that bind to THC. Once securely in place, THC kicks off a series of cellular reactions at the level of neurotransmitters that ultimately lead to the high that users experience when they smoke marijuana.

So what is the prevalence of use of Marijuana? The United Nations Drug Control Policy World Drug Report estimates that cannabis is the most widely abused illegal drug in all parts of the world, with around 141 million people, in total, consuming it. This corresponds to 2.45 percent of the world population. In particular, large numbers of young people experiment with cannabis. The proportion of school children and young adults who have used cannabis in the past-month can be as high as 10-25 per cent, and of those who have used it at least once in their lives is as high as 37 per cent in some countries. Globally, overall, cannabis abuse is increasing in many countries while stabilizing in countries where it has already reached high levels. There is additional concern that the new member countries of the European Union are seeing increased drug trafficking, escalating drug use in the new member states, and also a corresponding spread of infectious diseases.

According to the U.N. World Drug Report, the cannabis market remains buoyant with increasing consumption of marijuana in South America, and expanding markets in Western and Eastern Europe as well as in Africa.

Marijuana use hit its highest levels in America 1979 (a high of past month use of 13.2 percent for ages 12 and over in 1979.) Since then, use has dropped considerably. Marijuana hit a low in past month use in 2007 (5.8 percent for ages 12 and over), but began to rise again with the new emphasis on medical marijuana and marijuana legalization (to 7.3 percent in 2012 for ages 12 and over.)

As more people learn the truth about marijuana, the prevalence of use does continue to decrease. Also, as people age they naturally quit, or quit with assistance from treatment programs or Marijuana Anonymous (a 12 Step Fellowship support group.) Marijuana use drops to 4.1 percent for people age 26 and older, and drops again to 1.1 percent of the population for those over age 50. This is an important finding. The true prevalence of marijuana use is not anywhere near the cry of the marijuana proponents who say that it should be legalized because "everyone uses marijuana."

Of those who have used it even once, a significant percentage have quit never to use marijuana again. Overall, marijuana use in America tends to be correlated to age and decreases to less than one percent of the population as age increases beyond the youthful and young adult years and into adult years and then the senior years. In this regard then, note that marijuana use does not have the support of the majority of Americans by virtue of actual use, and in fact, is a behavioral phenomenon specific to a small group—and/or subgroup of the population. However, again, pro-marijuana advocates would have us believe otherwise and in fact are trying to aggressively change the social norms. They also release spurious opinion polls and biased surveys "proving" an overwhelming support for marijuana that in truth is just not there.

The consumption of marijuana is not recommended. For many users it causes mild-to-severe distress and it may have even more profound physical or psychological effects especially for the following: to individuals who are engaging in activities that could potentially place themselves and others at risk for personal injury such as operating machinery, use of firearms, swimming, boating, driving, etc.; to women who are pregnant or trying to conceive; to people who have a family history of chemical dependency (especially children of addicted parents); to individuals using other drugs including alcohol and/or prescription medications (even over the counter brands); to all individuals who are predisposed to emotional and mental issues and problems; to all children and adolescents; and to individuals who demonstrate some degree of chemical dependency on any substance.

Several of the major findings about marijuana use are startling:

— According to the Drug Abuse Warning Network, more than 455,000 patients entered emergency rooms with marijuana in their system in 2011, a 19% increase from just two years earlier according to government statistics.

— According to the Department of Health and Human Services TEDS (Treatment Episode Data Set), in 2011 there were 333,578 admissions of people into drug treatment programs who stated that marijuana was their primary drug of addiction. When included as a secondary or tertiary drug of choice, the number admitted into treatment is higher by tens-of-thousands of admissions.

— According to a major study of motor vehicle collision victims in a regional Trauma Unit near Toronto, marijuana was the most commonly found drug in impaired drivers other than alcohol and is growing.

— Marijuana is found to be a "gateway drug" and often leads to harder drugs. One study demonstrated that more than 60% of marijuana users progress to harder drugs (while the odds for non-users are only 1 percent!)

— According to a study published in the American Journal of Psychiatry, marijuana smokers are four times more likely to report symptoms of depression—including suicidal thoughts—as compared to those who never used the drug.

— According to a recent University Hospital study, adolescents who were heavy users of marijuana exhibited changes in their brain similar to those found in schizophrenics. Researchers conducted brain scans on male teenagers who were daily, long-term users of marijuana, as well as adolescent schizophrenia patients who did and did not use marijuana. They found that a region of the brain called the arcuate nucleus—which plays a role in higher cognitive function—was atrophied in both the marijuana users and those with schizophrenia. The study may lend credence to another finding of scientists that marijuana use can trigger schizophrenia.

There are scores of scientific studies that prove that marijuana is a harmful, addictive drug. As with alcohol and all drugs, marijuana can certainly lead to profound, chronic and progressive chemical dependency. Marijuana is currently up to 25 times more potent than it was in the sixties making the drug even more addictive, and many say that quitting marijuana is much more difficult than they thought (even more "difficult than quitting cocaine".)

Research has consistently demonstrated that there are *potentially* serious and damaging physical effects from marijuana use and abuse. There is documented evidence that marijuana typically causes acute changes in the heart and circulation. It increases the work of the heart, usually by raising the heart rate by as much as 50%, and in some people by raising blood pressure. While these effects may only be temporary, it increases the need for oxygen to the body while at the same time decreasing the supply of oxygen. This places a threat for persons with hypertension, cerebrovascular disease, and coronary arteriosclerosis. Research indicates that it may be especially dangerous for cardiac patients to combine marijuana with alcohol, which is a common occurrence. In fact, the National Academy of Science Institute of Medicine recommends that persons with cardiovascular disease avoid the drug entirely.

Smoking marijuana can lead to worse results for the lungs than smoking tobacco. There is nearly five times more carbon monoxide and three times as much tar inhaled into the lungs when one smokes a marijuana cigarette as opposed to a tobacco cigarette. Marijuana smokers may suffer bronchitis, emphysema, and bronchial asthma. Marijuana users are twice as likely to report symptoms of chronic lung disease as non-users, and one finding showed that men who smoked only marijuana on a regular basis displayed airway obstruction. Marijuana smoke produces 50% more hydrocarbons than tobacco smoke; and hydrocarbons are the chemicals associated with lung cancer. In fact, marijuana smoke contains 50% more cancer causing materials than tobacco smoke, and has been linked to both pre-cancerous growths and to cancer. Newer research shows that marijuana use is tied to cancer rates among Maoris: Maoris have the world's highest lung-cancer rate, and heavy marijuana use is a primary suspect.

About one in five New Zealanders are regular users of marijuana. Researchers in Wellington, New Zealand, are working on a study that compares cancer rates between marijuana smokers, tobacco smokers, and nonusers. They recently released a research review concluding that marijuana smoking is more cancerous than tobacco smoking. As a result, many are calling for a tougher approach than "harm reduction" to marijuana use in New Zealand.

Heavy use of marijuana may affect the endocrine or hormonal systems of both men and women causing reduced levels of testosterone, lowered sperm count, impotence, and gynecomastia (development of the mammary glands) in men, and disrupted menstrual cycles in women. Furthermore, high doses over a period of time can lead to depression of libido and impotence. In both animal and human studies, heavy use of marijuana was found to possibly interfere with the T-lymphocyte part of the immune system, reducing resistance to viral infection and cancer. Cannabis can also inhibit the intracellular synthesis of proteins, DNA and RNA, and inhibit cell division, similar to alcohol and the opioids.

In terms of school and academic success, studies have found that college students who use marijuana regularly had impaired skills related to attention, memory and learning twenty-four hours after they had last used the drug, suggesting that marijuana users may be limiting their ability to learn. Evidence especially shows that heavy marijuana smoking impairs the cognitive processes. Heavy marijuana users when compared to non-users show impaired cognitive functioning across the board, with significant impairment both in mathematics (a measure of the ability to do quantitative thinking) and in verbal expression (a measure of correct and appropriate word use.)

Using marijuana in college may increase the risk of leaving school. Researchers found that even students who only used marijuana occasionally were more likely to leave than their peers who did not use drugs. The study included 1,133 college students, who were followed over four years. The researchers found students who used marijuana more than 17 days a month were twice as likely as those who used marijuana less than a day per month to have an enrollment gap while in college. Students who used marijuana three to twelve days a month were more likely to have an enrollment gap, compared with those who did not use marijuana. “We wanted to look at whether or not drug use interferes with goals students had set for themselves. Our results show that marijuana use is not a benign thing," said lead researcher Dr. Amelia Arria, Director of the Center on Young Adult Health and Development at the University of Maryland School of Public Health. The findings appear in the Journal of Studies on Alcohol and Drugs.

In one study, heavy users showed a trend toward impairment in selecting synonyms, in literary comprehension, or overall ability to learn (not just when "high," but a lingering loss of cognitive skills after the euphoric effects wear off.) Animal studies show structural damage to the hippocampus, a structure critical in learning and memory, from the principle ingredient in marijuana (THC). A major study in New York demonstrated that 51 percent of marijuana using college students engaged in some form of "public misconduct" and 37 percent of users reported "serious personal problems" due to marijuana use.

In terms of employment, employees who are marijuana users were found less likely to commit to their organizations, had less faith in management, and experienced more job dissatisfaction. These workers reported more absenteeism, tardiness, accidents, worker's compensation claims, and job turnover than workers who did not use marijuana. They were also more likely to report to work with a hangover, miss work because of a hangover, and be drunk or use other drugs at work.

In one study, employees who tested positive for marijuana had 55% more industrial accidents and 85% more injuries compared to those that tested negative on a pre-employment exam, and they had absenteeism rates 75% higher than those that tested negative.

In terms of crime, marijuana use is definitely related to an increase in crime. In Omaha, 42% of all males arrested in 1995 tested positive for marijuana; in San Diego 35% of males arrested tested positive; and in Chicago 41% of arrestees tested positive for marijuana. In fact, the percentage of male arrestees testing positive for marijuana was equal to or greater than that of cocaine in 13 of 23 Drug Use Forecasting cities studied. In 2002, the National Institute of Justice's Arrestee Drug Abuse Monitoring (ADAM) Program, which collects data on the number of adult arrestees testing positive for various drugs, found that, on average, 41 percent of adult male arrestees and 27 percent of adult female arrestees tested positive for marijuana. On average, 57 percent of juvenile male and 32 percent of juvenile female arrestees tested positive for marijuana. It is important to note that these are not arrests for simple possession, but for crimes committed while intoxicated with or under the influence of marijuana.

Long-term marijuana use can certainly lead to marijuana dependency. According to both the American Psychiatric Association and the World Health Organization, the symptoms of marijuana dependence include increased tolerance, loss of control over predictable use, long term inability to cut down or stop, pre-occupation with obtaining or use of the drug, and less time devoted to family, school, work and recreation. The classic definition of addiction includes tolerance, withdrawal, loss of control, unsuccessful attempts to control use, craving, pre-occupation with use, use despite adverse consequences (continued use despite psychological, social, legal, familial, or personal consequences), and/or use despite resolution to quit or abstain. From any and/or all of these perspectives, *marijuana is a drug of addiction.*

According to the Department of Health and Human Services, in 2004, 4.5 million users of marijuana were classified with dependence on, or abuse of, marijuana (as opposed to recreational or incidental use.) As with alcohol and all drugs, marijuana can certainly lead to chronic and progressive chemical dependency.

Of course, psychological dependence on marijuana is much more common than physical addiction. With psychological dependency people trying to quit often report irritability, difficulty sleeping, and anxiety. Users display an increase in aggression on psychological tests, peaking approximately one week after they used. Pre-occupation with the drug and the associated lifestyle remain daily factors that those striving for abstinence must deal with.

While tolerance to marijuana and psychological dependency on marijuana are commonly accepted, some heavy users of marijuana certainly show signs of physical withdrawal. Physical dependence on cannabis may develop in those who use high doses daily, and abrupt termination of use can produce a withdrawal syndrome, with symptoms including sleep disturbance, irritability, loss of appetite and consequent weight loss, nervousness, anxiety, sweating, and upset stomach, chills, increased body temperature and tremors. The withdrawal sickness usually lasts for less than a week, although the sleep disturbances may persist for a longer period.

One treatment program demonstrated that two-thirds of cannabis-dependent patients reported withdrawal, and most claimed serious problems from the cannabis. Progression from first use to regular cannabis use was found as rapid as tobacco progression, and more rapid than that of alcohol, suggesting that for this population—that the drug potently reinforces cannabis-taking, producing both dependence and withdrawal.

As for the strength of marijuana dependence, many dependent users state that it is “impossible” for them to quit. In a study including people who use both cocaine and marijuana, many stated that giving up the use of marijuana was in some ways more difficult than giving up the cocaine use.

In all, it is estimated that about 10% of marijuana users become chemically dependent upon the drug during their years of heaviest use. As legalization grows, accessibility and availability expands, and potency increases this proportion will increase as well.

With treatment and a good 12-Step program people can and do recover and live a sober and clean life. Dependent people are strongly encouraged to access the available programs in their region, and government should make more prevention and treatment programs available and affordable—especially to those within the criminal justice and human service delivery systems.

Treatment includes counseling, support, and providing education and information about both the drug problem and the recovery process. Treatment programs are designed to motivate the patient to stop using marijuana, to identify situations that could increase the risk of relapse, to identify personal symptoms of dependency and to teach the skills needed to lead a substance free life. Treatment really offers the only choice for those who may want to stop the negative consequences of their drug use, and improve the quality of their lives.

While many researchers believe that marijuana is a mildly physiological addictive substance (on a scale of drugs with addiction potential, marijuana may not seem as physically addicting as heroin, crack or methamphetamine), studies do indicate that marijuana is harder to kick than many suspect and once developed—is as powerful as other drug addictions. In fact, marijuana is significantly more potent than it was in the sixties, making the drug even more addictive. In 1994, a U.S. Court of Appeals ruled that marijuana should remain a Schedule I drug as it is highly addictive.

Finally, here are some direct comments by former marijuana users themselves. It is interesting that often the denial system only breaks down after a person quits using marijuana and has some help to reflect back on his or her past and develop a self-awareness into his or her history of use. There are tens-of-thousands of these stories shared by former marijuana users.

One former marijuana user said he woke up one day and found that he was thirty years old and had wasted away his life and had nothing to show for it, so he “had to quit.”

Another user told of how marijuana made him become extremely paranoid and self-conscious. He didn’t want to deal with people so he would close his door, light up, and get high. For him, hitting bottom came after realizing that his life wasn’t going anywhere. He didn’t have any friends, felt awful, and wasn’t happy. So after eight years of smoking pot he realized he was looking for something that he could never get from marijuana and so he choose to quit.

One high school student started using marijuana because that was what his new “cool” friends were into, but then found that the next three years were filled with disappointments, lows, and superficial friendships. He became sad and depressed, but still couldn’t quit until he was arrested twice, lost his license, and then finally admitted he needed help and went into Marijuana Anonymous. Since then, his attitude, actions and direction in life have all changed for the better.

One fourteen year old began using pot and went through “two years of hell.” Like everyone else, he began by smoking just on occasion. He didn't see that marijuana began to control his life. His relationship with his parents began to turn negative, and he began to treat them as if they were idiots and he was in constant battles with his parents and siblings, often hurting them. His grades dropped to a 1.6 grade point average. He began dealing, and he was arrested. Finally, after everything "hit the fan," he got help and immediately noticed vast improvements in his life and relationships—which only continue to get better. He hasn't used marijuana since then, and understands now that marijuana made him think he was the most important person in the world and he sees that at the time it made him become self-centered and selfish.

# BRAIN CHEMISTRY AND PSYCHOPHARMACOLOGICAL PROPERTIES

The marijuana plant contains more than 400 different chemical compounds many of which are either toxic or poisonous to human life. There are at least 85 different cannabinoids isolated from cannabis unique to the plant, exhibiting varied effects. The main psychoactive or mind-altering ingredient is delta-9-tetrahydrocannabinol, THC.

Scientists have learned a great deal about how THC acts in the brain to produce its many effects. When someone smokes marijuana, THC rapidly passes from the lungs into the bloodstream which carries the chemical to organs throughout the body including the brain.

All drugs, including marijuana, change the way the brain works. To send messages in the brain, the brain cells or neurons release chemicals called neurotransmitters. Neurons are separated by tiny gaps called synapses. The neurotransmitters from one neuron move across the synapse and lock into spaces called receptors on other neurons. This starts an electro-chemical impulse in the receiving neuron, which then releases its own neurotransmitter. This entire process of brain chemistry, however, is altered by drugs.

In the brain, THC connects to specific sites called cannabinoid receptors on nerve cells and thereby influences the activity of those cells. Some brain areas have many cannabinoid receptors while others have few or none. Many cannabinoid receptors are found in the parts of the brain that influence pleasure, memory, thought, concentration, sensory and time perception, and coordinated movement such as the Cerebellum (important for body movement coordination), the Hippocampus (important for learning and memory), the Cerebral Cortex (especially the cingulate frontal, and parietal regions—important for the higher cognitive functions), the Nucleus Accumbens (important for the reward system), and the Basal Ganglia (important for movement and control). The brain regions in which cannabinoid receptors are moderately concentrated include the Hypothalamus (site of the body's housekeeping functions—body temperature regulation, salt and water balance, reproductive functions, etc.), the Amygdala (important for one's emotional response), the Spinal Cord (important for peripheral sensation, including pain), the Brain Stem (sites for sleep and arousal, temperature regulation, motor control, etc.), the Central Gray ( important for analgesia), and the Nucleus of the Solitary Tract (important for visceral sensation, nausea and vomiting.)

Marijuana affects the production or effect of certain neurotransmitters including dopamine, and norepinephrine. Serotonin and GABA levels may also be altered, as well as anandamide. One of the most important chemicals it affects is glutamate, a chemical researchers know is vital for learning, memory, storage of information and processing of that information. In one recent study, scientists found that marijuana use prevented the formation of new synapses of hippocampal neurons, and this may be the mechanism that contributes to the impairment of memory produced by cannabinoids.

Marijuana is a psycho-active drug, a very powerful, mind and mood altering drug. A very small amount of cannabis, i.e. containing 2-to-3 mg of THC, can produce a high for the occasional user. Studies show that a single marijuana cigarette may contain 20-30 mg and some joints may contain as much as 500 milligrams of marijuana. A 'blunt' may have 3000 milligrams. Marijuana can also be mixed into foods, such as brownies, or brewed as a tea. Different types of these food preparations are growing by the day and are known as edibles or Marijuana Infused Products (MIPs). Sometimes another drug is added to the mixture, such as crack cocaine, PCP, or methamphetamine. Of course most marijuana users also drink alcohol, and this poses additional problems and effects.

When THC, also a cannabinoid chemical, binds with cannabinoid receptors, it activates neurons and influences cell activity which causes adverse effects—*abnormal effects*—on the mind and body. For instance, when the THC binds with the cannabinoid receptors inside the hippocampus, it interferes with the recollection of recent events or time perception. THC also affects coordination, which is controlled by the cerebellum. The basal ganglia controls unconscious muscle movements, which is another reason why motor coordination is impaired when under the influence of marijuana.

THC is just one of some 85 cannabinoids, but it's the chemical most often associated with the effects that marijuana has on the brain. Cannabis plants also contain choline, eugenol, guaicacol and piperidine. The concentration of THC and other cannabinoids varies depending on growing conditions, plant genetics and processing after harvest.

THC is a very potent chemical compared to other psychoactive drugs. It has been reported that an intravenous (IV) dose of only 1 milligram can produce serious mental and psychological effects. Once in your bloodstream, THC typically reaches the brain within seconds after it is inhaled and begins to have its effects.

Most frequently, the marijuana high usually lasts two or three hours, during which a wide range of varying effects may occur. The most usual effect is an intensification of "sensation" and "perception." The user may experience vivid colors, or more depth or patterns in vision. Other senses may be intensified, sounds can be more distinct or music more defined. Smell and taste seem more enhanced with marijuana. Even skin receptors seem more affected with heat, cold, and touch as more sensitive. Researchers found that pain can have a contradictory effect. If one is not concentrating on the area of pain there is a reduced sensitivity to it, but if there is great awareness of pain from an injury it can last for a longer time with greater intensity and quality of pain with marijuana use. Other feelings and sensations and stimulations may have greater distinction. These sensations may vary considerably in quality and intensity depending upon the individual and circumstances. Sometimes one will focus on a particular sensation virtually to the exclusion of others, and at other times nothing will seem to happen.

As a pseudo-euphorohallucinogen, the effects of this drug may vary widely and are particularly sensitive to individual differences in personality and environmental settings. At moderate-to-high doses of THC, mood varies considerably while anxiety and panic have often been reported. Depression may also be enhanced. Impairment of short term memory, disturbances in thought patterns, lapses in attention, depersonalization, and sensory distraction also occur. Larger doses can bring on stronger distortions of time and space, illusions, mental confusion and panic reactions. Extremely large doses can cause hallucinations, and marijuana flashbacks have been reported by some users. Depending on dose and type, euphorohallucinogens variously produce hypoactivity or hyperactivity, aggression or docility, marked autonomic stimulation, incoordination, and hypersensitivity to sensory stimuli. These compounds alter the electroencephalogram tests in both animals and humans.

THC interferes with the normal functioning of the cerebellum, the hippocampus and portions of the cerebrum. Animal studies have shown an accumulation of THC stored in the synaptic vesicles of the brain cells. This results in a thickening of the cell wall and synaptic cleft (perhaps hundreds of times thicker than normal). Ultimately, this can profoundly slow the transmission of neurotransmitters and causes interference of the delivery at the receptor site.

While the most notable cannabinoid is the phytocannabinoid THC as the primary psychoactive compound of cannabis, cannabidiol (CBD) is another major constituent of the plant, representing up to 40% in extracts of the plant resin. Cannabidiol (CBD) is not psychoactive. It appears to relieve convulsion, inflammation, anxiety, and nausea, and may relieve psychotic symptoms. In effect, research may be showing that CBD and not THC has the medicinal properties desired through marijuana. Research is continuing to explore this further.

Cannabinoids can be administered by smoking, vaporizing, oral ingestion, transdermal patch, intravenous injection, sublingual absorption, or rectal suppository. Once in the body, most cannabinoids are metabolized in the liver. Some is also stored in fat in addition to being metabolized in the liver. Delta-9-THC is metabolized to 11-hydroxy-delta-9-THC, which is then metabolized to 9-carboxy-THC. Some cannabis metabolites can be detected in the body several weeks after use. These metabolites are the chemicals recognized by drug tests but do not represent ongoing intoxication, but rather molecules that accumulate in the fatty tissues from past use.

Thus, marijuana has the most direct impact upon brain chemistry and the pathways of brain chemicals. Brain chemistry is a very sensitive and delicately balanced process, and is not one open to interference or manipulation without serious long term negative effects. To increase or decrease these chemicals, or to alter the functioning of the nerve cells or receptor sites in any way can result in long term impairment and dysfunction, whatever the cause. It is not uncommon to see at the very least, marijuana users present themselves in the emergency rooms with a host of disorders from anxiety and apprehension to full depersonalization, to even delusions or hallucinations, which are simply the direct results of altered brain chemistry. Brain chemistry is delicate and fragile and not amenable through alteration. The term that used to be used for this syndrome long term, was called "Burn Out."

# MARIJUANA AND MENTAL ILLNESS

Research has long implicated cannabis as an exacerbating factor in mental illness, and most especially where mental illness and/or personality problems are pre-existing or concurrent conditions. Recent research has largely supported these earlier findings and also implicates a role of marijuana with anxiety disorders, mood disorders, depression and other areas of mental illness.

As important to note, however, is that there is now sound evidence that taking cannabis leads to acute adverse mental effects in a high proportion of regular users. While it was known that many of these adverse symptoms were related to constitutional factors including youthfulness, personality attributes, and vulnerability to serious mental illness, research now shows that the effects of marijuana as a causative factor for mental illness are based upon effects which are dose-related, and include potency and frequency of use.

One study found that the severity of depression, anxiety and alexithymic symptoms increased progressively with the degree of involvement with cannabis, and chronic use of cannabis was associated with a high prevalence of co-morbid psychiatric disorders. Other studies demonstrated that cannabis use predicted an increased risk of developing clinical psychosis, and cannabis users showed higher scores on schizotypy, borderline and psychoticism scales than never-users; that the risk of developing schizophrenia among heavy users was six times greater than among non-users; that for highly introspective individuals, marijuana use was associated with self-reports of poorer adult mental health; that greater dependence on alcohol and marijuana was found to be one determining factor predicting worse outcomes for youth in areas of criminality, conduct disorder, depression, and attention-deficit/hyperactivity disorder; and that substance dependence (including cannabis) related significantly to suicide attempts and self-injury histories of youth. Other studies have implicated marijuana use in depression, panic reactions, suicide, and anti-social personality characteristics.

The American Psychiatric Association demonstrates the seriousness and severity of marijuana effects beyond simple cannabis intoxication. Diagnostic categories include Cannabis Intoxication Delirium, Cannabis Induced Psychotic Disorder with Delusions, Cannabis Induced Psychotic Disorder with Hallucinations, Cannabis Induced Anxiety Disorder, and Cannabis Related Disorders not Otherwise Specified. The Cannabis related mental disorders are quite serious, and many people find themselves as chronic clients in mental health programs or as mentally ill chemical abusers because of the effects of marijuana. In fact, early use of marijuana has been shown to double the risk of someone developing schizophrenia and other psychoses—including mania and bipolar disorder—and mood disorders. Also, it can worsen psychotic symptoms for those already ill, and trigger relapse. Several studies support this finding.

Less dramatic, but also troubling, are effects of cannabis on acute or chronic impairment of attention, memory and psychomotor performance. These effects can contribute to reduced functioning and quality of life, as well as an increase in accidents and day-to-day injuries.

The effects of smoking marijuana typically cause decreased activity in the posterior temporal lobes bilaterally within the brain. The damage can be mild or severe, depending on how long a person used, how much use occurred, the degree of potency of the drug, what other substances were used in conjunction, and how vulnerable a particular brain is.

Brain scans show that, normally, in the healthy brain of a non-marijuana user blood flow to the brain is good. Compared to scans of heavy marijuana smokers, scans show "pits and disruptions" where there is poor or no blood flow in the brain. This can have a dramatic effect on behavior, depending on which area of the brain is affected. Often these behavioral changes will be blamed on a psychological problem, when, in fact, there is a genuine biological basis for them—a basis caused by marijuana abuse.

This often comes as a shock to those who do not believe cannabis damages the brain. Cannabis squeezes down blood flow leading to brain cell damage and death. In the Amen clinic, Dr. Daniel Amen's research has found that it particularly affects the temporal lobes—the area responsible for memory. Dr. Amen suggests that this is the reason for the poor memory and lack of motivation that chronic marijuana users often report.

There are many other studies that show negative effects on the brain, on cognitive skills, and on maturation and brain development. In Ireland, the number of children treated for mental disorders caused by smoking cannabis has quadrupled since the government downgraded the legal status of the drug.

Regular marijuana use increases the risk of developing serious mental illness. As reported in the National Survey on Drug Use and Health (NSDUH) 2005 report, the younger a person is when they begin to use marijuana the more likely they are to develop serious mental illness in their lifetime. The report shows that more than 2,250,000 adults aged 18-to-25, who reported lifetime marijuana use, developed serious mental illness: 10.5% (almost 240,000) started using marijuana at age 18 or older; and fully twice as many, 21% (more than 450,000) started before the age of 12. This report clearly indicates a correlation between marijuana use and the development of serious mental illness, with the risk being higher for early age-of-onset of use.

Another study suggests marijuana may accelerate the onset of (early) psychotic disorders in some young users. Researchers at the University of New South Wales in Sydney, along with investigators at two U.S. sites, conducted an exhaustive review of the literature examining the effects of marijuana, alcohol, and other drugs on the onset of psychiatric disorders such as schizophrenia. Eighty-three studies involving more than 22,000 patients met inclusion criteria. Past research has shown that one in every 100 Americans develops schizophrenia in his or her lifetime, with symptoms typically surfacing in the late teens or early 20s for men and in the late 20s and early 30s for women. The researchers found patients with psychotic disorders who smoked marijuana at an early age developed symptoms almost three years sooner than those who did not. The link was strongest among those who started smoking at ages 12-to-15. These results strengthen the link between marijuana and the development of psychiatric diseases, and may even point to a causal relationship for some users, according to Michael T. Compton, M.D., a behavioral scientist at George Washington University Medical Center in Washington, DC, and a coauthor of the paper. The study was published in the February 2011 Archives of General Psychiatry.

Marijuana use is now linked to a decline in I.Q. Researchers at Carleton University in Ottawa, compared the IQ scores of 74 participants who took IQ tests between the ages of 9-and-12 and then again between the ages of 17-and-20. Participants were tested for drug use throughout the study period. The researchers found that participants who smoked five-or-more marijuana cigarettes a week had a decline in their IQ scores compared to the test results taken in their preteen years. The study is published in the May 2002 issue of the Canadian Medical Association Journal. Another study in the journal National Proceedings of the Academy of Sciences stated that teens who smoke marijuana see their IQs drop as adults, and deficits persist even after quitting according to a another study. A smoker's I.Q. may drop, on average, 8 points.

Adolescents and young adults who are heavy users of marijuana were found to be more likely than non-users to have disrupted brain development ("Diffusion Abnormalities in Adolescents and Young Adults with a History of Heavy Cannabis Use", Ashtari, M., Cervellione, K., Cottone, J., Ardekani, B.A., Kumra, S., Journal of Psychiatric Research, January 2009.)

In February, 2010, researchers at Queensland Brain Institute and School of Population Health reported results of a study which began in the early 1980s. In the study, a group of 3800 children born in a Brisbane, Australia hospital were followed for almost 30 years. Results of this study offered some of the most credible and convincing evidence to date. *Those who began marijuana use at an early age were three times more likely to suffer from some form of psychotic disorders by the time they reach the age of 21, including hallucinations, psychosis, delusions, and schizophrenia.*

Research suggests that delta-9-THC, the principal active ingredient in marijuana, can cause transient schizophrenia-like symptoms, such as suspiciousness, unusual thoughts, paranoia, thought disorder, blunted affect, reduced spontaneity, reduced interaction with the interviewer, and problems with memory and attention. The study, led by D. Cyril D'Souza, M.D., professor of psychiatry at Yale School of Medicine, set out to explore a long-known association between cannabis and psychosis.

According to research presented at the annual meeting of the Radiological Society of North America (RSNA), heavy use of marijuana may put adolescents who are genetically predisposed to schizophrenia at greater risk of developing the brain disorder. Using a sophisticated brain imaging technique called diffusion tensor imaging (DTI), researchers at Zucker Hillside Hospital in Glen Oaks, New York, drew these conclusions from their study of the brains of groups of adolescents: healthy, non-drug users; heavy marijuana smokers (daily use for at least one year); and schizophrenic patients.

One study using a MRI technique, mapped the structural integrity of brain tissue in eleven heavy marijuana users and eleven age matched controls. The study found impaired structural integrity affecting the fibre tracts of the corpus callosum, suggesting the possibility that the structural abnormalities in the brain may underlie cognitive and behavioral consequences of long-term heavy marijuana use.

Another MRI study found that heavy cannabis users had an averaged 12 per cent volume reduction of the hippocampus, and a 7 per cent reduction of the amygdala compared to controls. In addition, the study found that long-term cannabis users suffered from psychotic experiences, such as persecutory beliefs and social withdrawal, in addition to the loss of memory equivalent to 15 additional years of aging.

Another study measured slow brain potentials in response to "Go" and "No Go" conditions before, during and after marijuana smoking. The study found normal responses both before and during smoking, but severely disrupted responses 20-40 minutes later.

Another study utilized BOLD MRI to examine the brain activation patterns in chronic marijuana users and matched control subjects during a set of visual attention tasks. The researchers found a reorganized visual-attention network and cerebellar hypoactivation associated with marijuana use. Although all subjects demonstrated similar task and cognitive test performance, active and abstinent marijuana users showed decreased activation in the right prefrontal, medial and dorsal parietal, and medial cerebellar regions (regions affected by THC), but greater activation in various frontal, parietal and occipital brain regions. Investigators hypothesized that marijuana users had lost some functionality in parts of the brain affected by marijuana use, which was compensated for by other regions of the brain.

A study by the RAND policy research group found that marijuana smokers had lower math scores than non-users. "It makes a lot of sense that marijuana would affect certain types of cognitive functioning, particularly things that are hard to grasp, like math," said Rosalie Pacula, an economist with RAND who led the study. Pacula analyzed 6,000 standardized test scores of students who started using marijuana after the 10th grade and compared them with results when they were in the 12th grade. The research showed that students who smoked marijuana had 15 percent lower scores in math than nonsmokers. Pacula said the lower math scores could translate to a 2 percent lower salary later in life. She presented her findings at an economics conference in San Francisco.

A study on laboratory rats hints that women who smoke marijuana during pregnancy may put their child at risk for lasting mental defects. For the study, Italian researchers injected pregnant rats with an artificial cannabis substance called WIN. The dosage represented that inhaled by a typical human smoker. The researchers then gave the rats' offspring learning tests. The researchers found that the offspring of the rats given WIN had lower memory-retention scores than rats whose mothers had not been given the substance. In addition, WIN had disrupted the release of a neurotransmitter called glutamate, as well as electrical activity associated with learning. "Memory impairment in prenatally WIN-exposed rats seems to be a persistent condition, present at both 40 and 80 days of age," said the researchers from the Italian universities of Cagliari, Ferrara, Bari, and Rome. "These findings could provide an explanation of cognitive alterations observed in children born from women who use marijuana during pregnancy." Marijuana is the most widely used illegal drug among women of reproductive age. The study's findings are published in the Proceedings of the National Academy of Sciences.

Another study found that teen drug use is related to psychological disorders later in life. The study by researchers at the Mount Sinai School of Medicine in New York tracked 736 people aged 14 to 27 for 14 years, the researchers determined that frequent use of alcohol, marijuana, and other illegal drugs during adolescence and early adulthood were linked to episodes of major depressive disorders, alcohol dependence, and substance-use disorders in the late 20s. "The fact that we are able to predict this is new, startling and alarming," said Dr. David W. Brook, a Mount Sinai psychiatrist and one of the authors of the study. *The previous belief was that psychological problems led to substance abuse, while this study clearly defines psychological problems are caused by substance abuse, including marijuana.*

Regular marijuana use increases the risk of developing serious mental illness as well as emotional and other psychological problems. As previously stated an analysis of the National Survey on Drug Use and Health (NSDUH) report shows that the younger a person is when they begin to use marijuana, the more likely they are to develop serious mental illness in their lifetime, and the earlier the age-of-onset of use the greater the likelihood of mental problems. As the effects of marijuana are dependent upon the set and setting of use, teens and adults who already have some degree of depression, emotional lability, or mental issues are even more vulnerable to cannabis-related mental illness. As well, the potency, dosage, and frequency of use are other factors which may predict future problems. Marijuana is a contributing factor to mood disorders, anxiety disorders, depression, dysthymia, mania, hypomania, panic, panic with agoraphobia, social phobias, generalized anxiety, schizophrenia and other forms of psychosis, etc. There is also some evidence that in vulnerable teens, because of genetic factors, the abuse of marijuana can trigger a schizophreniform disorder.

One of the most under-appreciated findings is that for teens and adults both, marijuana induced depression can certainly lead to suicidal ideation and even suicide itself.

The relationship of marijuana in mental illness is not a weak correlation. For tens-of-thousands it is a very serious causative factor of mental illness and one which people in recovery will honestly admit has caused them and their families a great deal of needless pain and suffering.

# MARIJUANA AND MATURATIONAL DEVELOPMENT

Adolescence is a crucial period of emotional and psychological development—of maturation. This stage of development includes the building of coping skills, anger management skills, stress management skills, patience, values and character. It is a period of formative years for puberty, for physical, sexual and emotional development, for personality, intellectual and social development, for responsibility and accountability. It is especially critical for brain development including the maturing of centers of the brain for reasoning, thinking and logic—for the higher cognitive functions.

One of the most misunderstood phenomena is adolescent development and the variables lending toward healthy and mature development. Adolescence is a time of life when mind and body are maturing, and when social and emotional mechanisms of adjustment are being formed. As use of marijuana generally begins during teen years, risk of impaired emotional growth and development is of crucial concern. Many psychiatrists have expressed concern that regular marijuana use by youth produces adverse effects on psychological maturation. It has long been said that emotional development ceases at the time one begins marijuana use. Although not definitive, studies have shown that marijuana use may increase the risk of discontinuing high school education and of increasing job instability in young adulthood, and of developing inability to follow-through or accept progressively higher responsibilities and progressive adult obligations. Thus, at the most critical point of life when these social skills are to be nurtured and developed, marijuana stunts them and prevents the progressive maturation into adulthood. These effects upon development may cascade throughout young adult life and impact upon the quality of life of the user as an adult, and even demonstrate long term dysfunction upon their future families and children.

New research attests to a dynamic called "compressed adolescence." Researchers today believe that heavy marijuana users skip over important social and emotional skill building experiences and grow to lack significant adult skills like appropriate anger management and confrontation techniques. This lack of building adult coping mechanisms and related emotional and social skills, creates serious long term quality of life problems for users.

Clinicians have often remarked that patients in their 30s have the maturation levels, emotional responses and reactions of teenagers. It is as if the marijuana use stunted the users psychological growth, leaving him/her with an underdeveloped maturation level seemingly commencing to the age of onset of marijuana use.

Psychologists argue that when a teen starts smoking marijuana heavily, they lose the ability to consolidate the emotional and social learning necessary for a real transition out of adolescence and into adulthood. Marijuana dulls the emotional response to external stimuli, and as such when under the influence of marijuana, teens do not experience complex emotional and developmental challenges in a normal appropriate manner and do not learn healthy ways to navigate the emotional and psychosocial landscape of adulthood. The earlier teens start smoking, the greater the deficit in learned social behaviors, and the greater the eventual harms.

Research presented at the American Academy of Pediatrics revealed that chronic, heavy marijuana use during adolescence is associated with poorer performance on thinking tasks including slower psychomotor speed and poorer complex attention, verbal memory and planning ability. While findings suggest partial recovery of verbal memory functioning within the first three weeks of adolescent abstinence from marijuana, complex attention skills continue to be affected. Females may be at increased risk for the neurocognitive consequences of marijuana use during adolescence, as studies found that teenage girls who use marijuana had marginally larger prefrontal cortex volumes associated with poorer executive functions of the brain, i.e. planning, decision-making or staying focused on a task.

At low doses, most marijuana users report a sense of calm, well-being and relaxation—the exact opposite of anxiety. According to an article in the Journal of Substance Abuse Treatment (June 2009), a person under the influence of marijuana becomes more emotional and sensitive and many times it increases stress, and according to other research decreases the capacity to cope with stress long term. Accordingly, young people who are weekly marijuana users double their risk of depression later in life.

A study by Brook, Adams, Balka, and Johnson, demonstrated an association between early marijuana use and outcome variables including lower educational and occupational expectations, being suspended or expelled from school, fired from jobs, getting "high" at school or work, collecting welfare, rebelliousness, not participating in productive activities, and being an unmarried parent. In an extensive study, "Cannabis

Use and Later Life Outcomes", Fergusson and Boden found similar results as well as overall lower satisfaction with relationships and lower life satisfaction.

In yet another study, adolescents and young adults who are heavy users of marijuana were found more likely than non-users to have disrupted brain development. Pediatric researchers found abnormalities in areas of the brain that interconnect brain regions involved in memory, attention, decision-making, language and executive functioning skills. The findings are of particular concern because adolescence is a crucial period for brain development and maturation. "Studies of normal brain development reveal critical areas of the brain that develop during late adolescence, and our study shows that heavy cannabis use is associated with damage in those brain regions," said study leader Manzar Ashtari, Ph.D., director of the Diffusion Image Analysis and Brain Morphometry Laboratory in the Radiology Department of The Children's Hospital of Philadelphia. The study appeared in the Journal of Psychiatric Research, January 2009.

While the research has been less clear on other areas of personality development with marijuana use (other than amotivational syndrome and the maturation process), two other areas of concern have surfaced. One researcher found that marijuana users tend to become hypersensitive to criticism and tend to over-react to any hint of criticism, constructive or otherwise. As criticism is a part of anyone's life, for instance a job performance review at work, this inability to accept and learn from criticism places one at higher risk of multiple problems—including quitting jobs, not being able to handle anger constructively, forming an inability to learn from one's mistakes, a decreased ability to change or otherwise adapt, and a formation of a reactive posture to life.

A second common finding, although anecdotal, reported by parents is that their children who use marijuana tend to be defiant and rebellious to family norms and customs. Now many researchers have failed to provide this causal linkage to the marijuana use for obvious reasons—they say that one cannot conclude that it is the marijuana causing this personality syndrome because it might just be typical adolescent behavior. Again, though, parents report that the change *became pronounced* once marijuana was introduced, similar to school grades dropping *after* marijuana use started. So while there always may be some testing of rules by teens, some level of striving for independence and functional autonomy, some level of age-appropriate rejection of family norms and customs, children usually mature and outgrow these characteristics—and in fact, eventually adopt their family's style of behavior and interaction. Clearly, however, the moods, attributes and behaviors associated with marijuana use have a different flavor and classification, and have become part of a signature pattern for marijuana users—especially those who still live at home.

According to a World Health Organization Report, the effects of adolescent marijuana use upon development may *"cascade throughout young adult life and impact upon the quality of life of the user (as an adult) and even upon their children."*

Clearly, many studies have concluded that marijuana use, especially early-onset during the formative years, presents a very real barrier to healthy growth, maturation and development. While it is generally accepted that marijuana use causes emotional stagnation, the question that remains to be answered is to what extent this causes a lifelong failure-to-thrive phenomena.

# MARIJUANA AND THE AMOTIVATIONAL SYNDROME

Perhaps one of the greatest misconceptions about marijuana is the lack of understanding about a causal effect of marijuana with the development of a particular pattern of thoughts, attitudes and behaviors commonly identified as an "amotivation syndrome." Stories of a marijuana related amotivational syndrome—where chronic and/or heavy cannabis use impairs motivation and social performance, have been described in societies with a long history of marijuana use such as Egypt, Greece, the Caribbean and elsewhere. With the increase of cannabis use among young adults in the USA in the late 1960s, reports of a similar syndrome occurring among heavy cannabis users began being identified here.

Clinical evidence suggests a correlation between chronic use of marijuana and the development of a syndrome characterized by a marked decrease in personal drive, motivation and ambition, with apathy about the future, lethargy, shortened attention span, high distractibility, decreased concentration, and an overall impairment of judgment and memory of the chronic user. This syndrome may not be unique to marijuana. There are several reports describing similar psychiatric disorders of an amotivational syndrome among patients with a history of other psychoactive substance use including solvents, methamphetamine, OTC cough syrups, and certain medications and drugs such as with Selective Serotonin Reuptake Inhibitors (SSRIs.) In this respect, it may be understood that substances with certain psychoactive properties may also share in certain pharmacological dynamics such as amotivational characteristics.

The true "evidence", however, comes from a plethora of anecdotal observations shared by both parents, school personnel, and professionals with opportunity to see and observe what can be best characterized as "dramatic" changes. The many stories include youth whose academic marks dropped significantly after the initiation of marijuana use; employees whose work performance suddenly suffered without other explanation; and an amotivational "signature" observed by clinicians in treatment programs. Most important, however, is the multitude of self-reports by former marijuana users. These self-reports clearly describe a syndrome that had developed post marijuana use and in many cases self-corrects with the cessation of marijuana smoking in concurrence with time (it seems that for a significant percentage of users only a period of time after achieving abstinence can remove the cerebral haze of marijuana effects, allowing a restoration of cognitive functioning.)

Researchers have found amotivational syndrome to be among the often reported co-occurring symptoms and disorders of chronic marijuana use (Research Report Series, "Marijuana Abuse—How Does Marijuana Use Affect Your Brain and Body?" National Institute on Drug Abuse.) In fact, severe amotivational syndromes, with the appearance of pseudodementia, have been reported in heavy users, in particular in countries where consumption is high. Although more pronounced, these syndromes are reminiscent of the lack of motivation observed in regular consumers. ("Cannabis: Effects of Consumption on Health", by INSERM—Institut National de la Santé et de la Recherche Médicale; French Institute of Health and Medical Research, 2001.)

One researcher documented this phenomena as "psychosocial dysfunction" resulting from repeated use of the substance which includes persistent procrastination, low productivity, low self-confidence, interpersonal or family conflicts, memory problems and financial difficulties where individuals often achieve considerably below their true potentials (Budney, A. J., & Moore, B. A., 2002, "Development and Consequences of Cannabis Dependence", Journal of Clinical Pharmacology, 42, 1S-6S; National Institute on Drug Abuse—2005, Marijuana Abuse [NIDA Research Report Series No. 05-3859], Bethesda, MD: U.S. Dept. of Health & Human Services.)

Hubbard, Franco, and Onaivi, reported that amotivational syndrome has been found to be one of the neuropsychiatric adverse effects of marijuana ("Marijuana—Medical Implications", American Family Physician, December 1999.)

In one study of 268 cannabis users, 21 percent interviewed stated that marijuana led to "tiredness, low motivation and lack of energy." ("Long-Term Cannabis Use: Characteristics of Users in an Australian Rural Area", Reilly D., Didcott P, Swift W. Hall W., Northern Rivers Health Service, Lismore, New South Wales, Australia, June 1998.)

According to Dr. Istvan Boksay, chief of psychiatry at the Aging and Dementia Research Center and a research pharmacologist at NYU Medical Center—the biochemical basis for this syndrome "is caused by the temporary low levels of testosterone produced by marijuana." Says Boksay, "You don't feel like doing much, with the exception of eating"

("Marijuana and Anti-depressants Don't Mix", Spotlight Health, January 24, 2001.)

Other studies demonstrate the occurrence of the syndrome as well. In one six-year study of 49 high school disciplinary hearings for students possessing or being under the influence of marijuana, it was found that all students had serious school attendance problems; all students were one or more years behind their classmates in academic progress towards graduation as a result of numerous class failures; those who at one time had been involved in sports or other extracurricular activities had dropped out once regular marijuana use began; and the teachers characterized all of the 49 students as apathetic and unmotivated (Zion-Benton Township High School, Zion, Illinois, "A Study of 49 Students Expelled for Marijuana Violations" 1999.)

According to Dr. Richard Boyum ("A Two-Edged Sword: Marijuana Use and College Students", SelfCounseling.com), a person with a marijuana induced amotivational syndrome basically decreases the frequency of doing things that need to be done but may be more unpleasant to do. This may include going to early classes or to classes that are hard or unappealing, or in accomplishing tasks that may simply be unenjoyable. This best describes the cause and effect of marijuana and amotivational syndrome in most categories. Unfortunately it also readily describes the basis of the "drop out of life" phenomena of marijuana users as it seems that for a significant percentage of users, harder or progressively more challenging chores, responsibilities, accountabilities and higher level tasks are forfeited and career development is further retarded as a direct result of marijuana effects on the brain.

It remains unclear whether the development of an amotivational syndrome is an effect of simple or chronic use of marijuana. It is also not clearly understood what percentage of users may develop the full syndrome or fall anywhere on the spectrum of the syndrome. Research also has not identified which conditions—pre-existing or otherwise, also contribute to, or intensify, the development of the syndrome.

Conservatively, it has been suggested that heavy use of marijuana may increase the likelihood of the development of the syndrome, and that the syndrome does reinforce the chronic use of marijuana (Drugs and Drug Abuse, A Reference Text, second edition, Addiction Research Foundation). It is also suspected that early onset of use by adolescents or teens may be a factor, and that frequency of use, duration of use, and pre-existing psycho-social factors—or genetic dispositions may be exacerbated by marijuana.

In any event, the amotivational syndrome needs to be accepted as a very real adverse and unwanted side effect of marijuana for a significant percentage of users. It neither should be dismissed as a non-existent concern, nor minimized as a minor effect, nor thought of as a dynamic that does self-correct with marijuana cessation.

Everyone has an inherent potential for growth and development, refinement and achievement. Anything that poses an impediment to this potential is as great a problem as any disease which limits physical growth and development. Marijuana use has been proven to be a causative factor in the development of a limitation to human maturation. As such, it remains that the only guaranteed prevention of this chemically induced developmental syndrome is the total abstinence from all marijuana use.

# MARIJUANA AND DEFENSE MECHANISMS

Chemical dependency clinicians are very familiar with the role and function of defense mechanisms in maintaining active addiction. The basic question asked about addicts is, "Why don't they see what is happening to them?" The answer is because they cannot. They have lost touch with reality. Very often, even family members and many of those immediately around the addict, themselves, cannot really see what is happening to the chemically dependent person because of defense mechanisms.

As the disease of addiction grows so does a person's defense mechanisms—a system of defenses that begin to form and grow to protect people from pain and to protect their growing dependency and need for drugs. In essence, this is a survival mechanism. It is found that the stronger the drug dependency and greater the level of related pain, the higher and more rigid the defenses become. Very often this whole process is unconscious to the addict as well as to the family members. Addicts may truly not know what is happening inside of themselves until the dependency and defenses and pain grow to such levels that finally they—and their families—actually become victims of their own defense mechanisms.

Perhaps some of the best work on defenses was presented by Dr. Vernon Johnson, an Episcopal priest and recovered alcoholic who devoted his life to family intervention. Johnson developed the concept of "crisis intervention" and believed that an alcoholic or addict did not need to "hit rock bottom" before recovery. He explored the role of defenses in protecting and maintaining the active addiction and introduced the concept of intervention to penetrate those defense mechanisms.

Johnson divided his findings into two sets of defense mechanisms: the chemically (drug) induced defenses, and the naturally occurring—albeit, drug exaggerated defenses.

The three basic, chemically induced defenses are: Blackouts, Euphoric Recall, and Repression. A blackout is defined as chemically induced period of amnesia. It is not to be confused with passing out or drinking or drug use to the point of unconsciousness. A blackout is present inability to remember something that was said or done while in the state of intoxication. It is a basic sign of tolerance and cellular adaptation to a drug, and indicates an "overdose" for one's level of tolerance. Euphoric recall is a term that describes how addicts remember excessive drinking or drugging episode, that is, "euphorically" or totally happily, and with gross distortion. *An important note is that there is no time a drug user is able to accurately recall events or circumstances, feelings or attitudes, or the negative consequences that happened while he/she was under the influence, yet, they go on believing firmly that they remember everything in complete detail and that there were no negative consequences or unhappy events.* Together, these constitute chemically induced "repression."

The second set of defense mechanisms that Johnson identified are those defenses everyone knows and uses to some degree. Here if one may argue with a spouse, he or she may rationalize, justify or minimize actions or feelings. Projection, blaming, accusing, judging, and intellectualizing are other defenses commonly used. Some of the other fifty defense mechanisms that Johnson identified include explanations, generalizing, arguing, questioning, denial, complying, withdrawing, evading or dodging the issue, defiance, arrogance, attacking, shouting, threatening, etc.

Again, these are defenses that every one may use from time to time depending upon circumstances and the degree of ego-protection needed. The difference is that for the addict these are found to be much more pronounced, impenetrable by simple logic, and dysfunctional in the level of protection of the chemical usage—and that includes the marijuana user as well.

One hallmark feature of the stage of dependency is that the stronger these defenses are, usually the stronger the level of dependency upon the drug is as well. They can reach almost a pathological level, *"He can't see what everyone else can see."*

A marijuana user may be out of touch with reality. Marijuana addiction is a disease and as much as any other addiction, it is a disease of insanity.

So, with marijuana abuse or addiction the denial or minimization of the use or negative consequences of drug use is not necessarily indicative of the absence of a problem. Rather, the habitual use of denial, minimization or other defenses in fact may paradoxically indicate that someone has a very real and serious dependency upon marijuana.

# CANNABIS *IS* A DESTRUCTIVE DRUG

One of the greatest fallacies being spread about marijuana is that it is not a toxic drug, and therefore it is “safer” than other drugs like alcohol or nicotine.

The truth is that numerous legitimate and scientific studies have proven otherwise. One study in particular clearly demonstrated two dynamics of marijuana use: that it is harmful across a spectrum of criteria, and that it is as harmful and “toxic” as most other drugs.

A major study in Great Britain, published in the prestigious medical journal Lancet in November of 2010, compared 20 different drugs against 16 categories of harm—either as harm to self or harm to society.

The study, *Drug Harms in the UK: A Multicriteria Decision Analysis* by Professors David J. Nutt, FMedSci, Leslie A. King, PhD, and Lawrence D. Phillips, PhD. on behalf of the Independent Scientific Committee on Drugs, sought to demonstrate that the proper assessment of the harms caused by the misuse of drugs can inform policy makers in health, policing, and social care. For the study, a multicriteria decision analysis (MCDA) model was applied to a range of drug harms in the UK.

Cannabis was found to be in the top eight of the twenty drugs studied, for drug harm to self and to society.

*The study found that cannabis was associated with some 15 of the 16 criteria of harm.*

There were strong findings for cannabis with economic costs to self and society, crime, drug related impairment of mental functioning, drug specific impairment of mental functioning, drug dependency, and drug related damage.

Cannabis was also found associated with family adversity, loss of relationships, injury, negative effects on the community, loss of tangibles (income, housing, jobs, educational achievements, criminal record, imprisonment, etc.), and drug related mortality (accidents, cancers, etc.)

A secondary finding from this study is that cannabis was found to be harmful not just to self—but also significantly so—to others. This finding directly contradicts marijuana folklore that cannabis use does not interfere with the rights, health, or quality of life of others.

While the study acknowledged that several drugs were definitely more harmful than cannabis, it clearly demonstrated that cannabis is not a benign substance and is a substance that has negative results across the spectrum of criteria used for measuring harm. These marijuana related harms translate into a real reduction in the quality of life for self, family and society. Research exposed the myth: marijuana is a harmful drug.

# THC POTENCY

One of the greatest problems with marijuana is that the potency has, and continues, to increase. This poses a confounding element in the accurate prediction of effects and/or adverse effects. Marijuana growers are consciously trying to increase the content of the drug's active ingredient, THC, and continue to increase the THC content as high as possible. New strains and hybrids of cannabis sativa, cannabis indica, and cannabis ruderalis are cultivated every day. At one point there were 635 different strains found with different attributes and effects. However, all strains are potent and as growers continue sophisticated cultivation and growing techniques to accomplish that very goal—marijuana is becoming even more potent.

The THC of the 1970s marijuana is, simply, not the THC of today. In 1972, the average THC potency was less than 1 percent. That rose to 3 to 4 percent in the 1990s, and averages almost 13 percent today while the most potent strains have a THC content of about 25 percent (although federal law enforcement officers have found marijuana with a potency of 37 percent.) Hash oil typically ranges from 60-85 percent, but may be as high in potency of 95 percent. The newest product is marijuana wax with potency between 82 percent and 99.7 percent pure THC.

Potency is often a misunderstood concept. It is rarely given its due outside of the pharmacological arena.

Here are three examples of common supplements that will help explain potency.

Vitamin D is a vitamin everyone needs for healthy, functional living. It is generally accepted that both teens and adults need about 600 International Units (IUs) per day. Most agree that it is hard to overdose on Vitamin D or to reach toxic levels, but too much Vitamin D can hurt you. According to the Institute of Medicine, above 4000 IUs per day could be harmful. Very high doses of vitamin D can raise your blood calcium level, causing damage to blood vessels, heart, and kidneys, and it can further interact with particular (heart) medications causing an abnormal heart rhythm. So Vitamin D is one example where a substance that actually is beneficial becomes suspect—even toxic—based upon a potency or dosage factor.

A second example is fluoride. Fluoride is a byproduct of the phosphate fertilizer industry that has been added to municipal water supplies in North America for decades to help fight dental decay and as a benefit to teeth. Low doses of up to 20 mgs. per day seem to be safe for most people. However, studies show that higher doses are unsafe and/or with longer use fluoride can cause a large number of health risks. Higher doses can weaken bones and ligaments, and cause muscle weakness and nervous system problems. Also some evidence exists that it can cause dental fluorosis, cancer, reduced IQs in children, hypothyroidism, skin rashes, gastric distress, headaches, bone disease or other types of toxicity. Certainly here is an example of a very common supplement which in low dose is not a concern whereas with higher potency or quantity can cause a number of reactions and adverse side effects—some perhaps very serious.

A third example is magnesium. Magnesium is required for the proper growth and maintenance of bones. Magnesium is also required for the proper function of nerves, muscles, and many other parts of the body. It is important in more than 300 chemical reactions that keep the body working properly. Magnesium is probably safe for most people in doses less than 350 mgs per day, but for some people it might cause stomach upset, nausea, vomiting, diarrhea, and other side effects. A magnesium build up in the body, however, can cause serious side effects including an irregular heartbeat, low blood pressure, confusion, slowed breathing, coma, and death. It also needs to be more closely monitored for pregnant women or women breastfeeding, for those with heart block, or for those with kidney disease and/or kidney failure.

The effects of all drugs, i.e. the qualitative and quantitative differences demonstrated, are based in large part upon potency—the affinity and efficacy of that drug. While higher potency is not an absolute for more side effects, for psychoactive substances potency is a primary causative factor of side effects (as is frequency of use, as is set and setting of use, prior experience, and even bio-genetic factors.)

With THC specifically, a study released through the British Journal of Psychiatry in 2009 demonstrated that people with a first episode of psychosis had smoked higher-potency cannabis, for longer and with greater frequency than those who did not develop the psychosis. The study also concluded that high potency cannabis is displacing traditional cannabis preparations in many countries.

Doctors have expressed concerns about the dangers of higher potency marijuana, expressing the problems related to the higher addictive potential of such a drug, and other dangerous behaviors including Driving While Under the Influence (DUI). The National Institute on Drug Abuse lists "distorted perceptions, impaired coordination, difficulty in thinking and problem solving, and problems with learning and memory" among the effects of marijuana intoxication. The site also references research that has associated chronic marijuana use with increases in anxiety, depression, suicidal thoughts, and schizophrenia. These tend to become more serious as potency increases.

In all cases, the marijuana industry is attempting—and is accomplishing—the production of more strains of marijuana and strains with a higher potency for maximum euphoria (intoxication). This then, is a real concern and this is what will continue to cause toxicity, higher rates of dysfunctional living, higher rates of health problems, and higher rates of dependency among uses.

In the least, there is much agreement that increased potency of any drug can cause unwanted effects. That is why potency of medications is so closely prescribed and monitored by physicians. For marijuana users potency is as important. Here, there is an increased risk of damage to the areas of the brain that controls memory and emotion, there is an increased risk of addiction, an increased risk for psychiatric, social, legal, emotional, and intellectual consequences, and even higher risk that eventual brain changes can even impair the user's ability to experience pleasure. Yet, given this background marijuana producers strive to continually create higher levels of THC potency and marijuana users blindly continue to follow the herd.

# SIDE EFFECTS OF MARIJUANA

One of the most poorly misunderstood—and poorly appreciated set of findings about marijuana use is the short and long term negative effects of use. It is easiest to understand and accept these findings, if one thinks about them as "side effects."

All drugs have unintended effects. In the world of pharmacology, they may be classified as serious adverse effects (SAE), adverse effects (AE), or side effects (SE.) In fact, with drugs the side effects can be more pronounced (and harmful) than any intended effect(s), which is why people are told not to use any medications without an assessment, evaluation and expressed prescription of a physician, and under strict dosage, frequency, purity and monitoring requirements.

Thus, when pro-marijuana enthusiasts insist that marijuana has no negative effects to self or others, they are ignoring or discounting the basic dynamics of pharmacologia, pharmacokinetics, and psychopharmacology (the branch of pharmacology dealing with the psychological effects of drugs.).

All drugs, including medicines, have side effects. People may or may not feel the side effects, and there is no way to know for sure if a drug will cause a specific side effect(s) for a specific individual. It may depend on how much of the drug one takes, how old a person is, how much he/she weighs, whether one is male or female, and what other health problems and sensitivities one may have. Older adults are more likely to experience side effects than younger adults. With psychoactive drugs including marijuana, the effects are even more idiosyncratic and include the set and setting of the user (the context of use, emotions, past history, the life situation, the current environment, past traumas, self-esteem levels, personality characteristics, the reasons for use, ego strength, any family history of chemical dependency, etc.) In effect, especially for psychoactive drugs the side effects can be more pronounced than anticipated, and may also change from use-to-use seemingly without rhyme or reason.

Thus, when physicians ask, "are there any medications you are allergic too?", he/she is attempting to limit the frequency or degree of drug reactions or side effects—many of which are very serious if not deadly. But even if a person has no general allergic reactions to a particular drug they may show some form of drug specific intolerance or hypersensitivity to other drugs like an anti-cholesterol. Consider the commercials on television for prescription medications. After a litany of possible adverse reactions, the review of all possible side effects leaves the viewer thinking he/she would never take that drug. In some cases as many as 100 different side effects have been reported with particular drugs.

All drugs have primary intended effects and all drugs have side effects, and all people are vulnerable to experiencing them—albeit some people experience more side effects than others and some people experience them in greater degree than others.

So, marijuana needs to be accepted as a drug, and as all drugs it too has side effects—short and long term effects other than the desired effect of euphoria/intoxication. In this sense, marijuana also needs to be understood to have iatrogenic effects. Iatrogenic refers to any adverse condition(s) in a patient/person resulting from "treatment" or therapy, i.e., medication. Thus, if someone is using marijuana to help alleviate mild depression, it may actually deepen that very depression over a course of time.

The side effects of marijuana use are not fabricated. They are genuine effects as reported by users, observed by health care practitioners, identified through research, or witnessed by close friends or family.

A person may experience few or many of these side effects and, again, some are minor and some severe. As reported, side effects of marijuana use (including marijuana related problems) include: ataxia; amotivational syndrome; apathy; chronic unemployment; lower I.Q.; anxiety; phobias; academic underachievement; family dysfunction; anger and rage; psychosis; clinical depression; emotional lability; schizophrenia; cancer; low job performance; lethargy; asthma; impotency; mood changes; lapses in concentration; distortions of time and space; mental confusion; hallucinations; depersonalization; isolation from friends and family; suicidal ideation; impairment of judgment; cognitive problems; dizziness; lack of coordination; rapid heartbeat; unusual thoughts or behaviors; paranoid reaction; amnesia; abdominal pain; nausea; fatigue; insomnia; seizure; dependency; withdrawal; addiction; etc. It may even contribute to lower libido, lower sperm count, impaired sexual performance and gynecomastia—effects no man desires. Just a few of the problems one finds include intergenerational reliance on government welfare programs and charities; DUI; rise in Medicaid costs; and a multitude of social problems.

According to WebMD, marijuana is possibly unsafe in that its use can cause side effects including dry mouth, nausea, vomiting, dry or red eyes, heart and blood pressure problems, lung problems, impaired mental functioning, headache, dizziness, numbness, panic reactions, hallucinations, flashbacks, depression, and sexual problems. The special precautions and warnings about marijuana use concern pregnancy and breast feeding where it may slow the growth of the fetus and is also associated with childhood leukemia. It is discouraged where there is heart disease as marijuana might cause rapid heartbeat and short-term high blood pressure. Cannabinoids in marijuana can weaken the immune system, which might make it more difficult for the body to fight infections. Long-term use of marijuana can make lung problems worse, and regular, long-term marijuana use has been associated with several cases of an unusual type of emphysema, a lung disease. Marijuana might make seizure disorders worse in some people. As marijuana affects the central nervous system it may also slow the central nervous system too much when combined with anesthesia and other medications during and after surgery (thus, medical professionals recommend complete abstinence from marijuana at least two weeks before surgery.)

WebMD also cautions about drug interactions, including major interactions (especially marijuana mixed with sedatives and CNS depressants including barbiturates, clonazepam (Klonopin), lorazepam (Ativan), phenobarbital (Donnatal), zolpidem (Ambien), and others, and Theophylline (which may interact with marijuana in a reduced effect of theophylline.) For moderate drug interactions, it is not recommended to use marijuana with disulfiram (Antabuse) which can cause agitation, trouble sleeping, and irritability; or with fluoxetine

(Prozac) which interacts with marijuana and may contribute to hypomania. Marijuana may even act with many drugs causing minor drug reactions, especially with warfarin (Coumadin) which can result in an increased chance of bruising and bleeding.

Marijuana is simply, not a safe drug and every year over 455,000 marijuana users are admitted into hospital emergency rooms because of marijuana side effects or marijuana related accidents or events. Marijuana is a drug. All drugs have side effects.

# MARIJUANA AND SUICIDE

*In an international report in Nationmaster, of the top 15 countries with the highest proportion of marijuana users 13 also have the highest rates of suicide!*

*The top fifteen countries for the highest rates of marijuana use (in order of highest rates to lowest) were: New Zealand; Australia; United States; United Kingdom; Switzerland; Ireland; Spain; Canada; Netherlands; Belgium; France; Italy; Greece; Germany; and Denmark.*

*The top thirteen countries which also have the highest marijuana use rates and suicide rates are: New Zealand (26.7 suicides per 100,000 people); Switzerland (17.9 per 100,000); Canada (15 per 100,000); Australia (14.6 per 100,000); United States (13.7 per 100,000); Belgium (10.4 per 100,000); France (10.3 per 100,000); Denmark (9.3 per 100,000); Ireland (8.8 per 100,000); Netherlands (6.8 per 100,000); United Kingdom (6.7 per 100,000); Germany (4.7 per 100,000); and Italy (4.3 per 100,000).*

The research literature has long demonstrated a link between marijuana use and illnesses such as depression, schizophrenia, and suicidal ideation. Beyond comorbidity, however, more recent research makes a stronger case that cannabis smoking itself is a causal agent in these areas. As reported in the "Link Between Marijuana and Mental Illness", one 16-year study showed that individuals who were not depressed and then used marijuana *were four times more likely to be depressed at follow-up.* Another study investigated changes over a 14-year period and found that marijuana use was a predictor of later major depressive disorder(s.) A third study over a 21-year period found that marijuana use was associated with depression, suicidal thoughts, and suicide attempts.

The use of marijuana is strongly linked with an increased rate of depression. It is understandable that cannabis use could lead to an increased risk of suicide through a number of different mechanisms, including neurobiological effects, development of mental health problems such as depression or psychosis, or experiencing social disadvantages (such as poor academic achievement, unemployment, or poor social functioning) and a "failure to thrive in life" that might result directly from cannabis use. Dr. Daniel K. Hall-Flavin, M.D., of Mayo Clinic states, "...there is also some evidence that adolescents who attempt suicide may be more likely to use marijuana than those who don't." A Netherlands study at the Behavioural Science Institute of Radboud University Nijmegen, indicates that for about two-thirds of the population, genetic vulnerability to depression can be triggered through marijuana use. The study concludes that marijuana use is not merely a form of self-medication, but can lead to depression for those genetically predisposed.

Marijuana and depression are a dangerous combination, and for those who are depressed instead of relieving the symptoms of depression marijuana use can actually make depression worse and lead to more serious mental health problems including suicide.

Studies have found that use of marijuana weekly, or more frequent, doubles a teenager's risk of depression and anxiety;

that teens who smoke marijuana at least once a month are three times more likely to have suicidal thoughts than non-users; and depressed teens are twice as likely (as non-depressed teens) to abuse or become dependent on marijuana. One report also shows that "girls who smoke marijuana daily" are five times more likely to "experience symptoms of depression and anxiety" than girls who do not smoke marijuana.

Another study involved close to 2,000 participants in the Baltimore area who were interviewed in 1980 and then again between 1994 and 1996. The researchers assessed the participants for signs of marijuana abuse and symptoms of depression. Researchers defined abusers of marijuana as people for whom the drug caused social problems, such as inability to perform at work. The results showed people who initially did not have depressive symptoms but abused marijuana were more than four times as likely to have depressive symptoms at the follow-up date than those who did not abuse marijuana. The depressive symptoms associated with earlier marijuana abuse included suicidal thoughts and a feeling of boredom.

Colorado has approved medical marijuana, and also recreational marijuana. Colorado now set an unfortunate record with the highest number of suicides ever recorded in state history—now at a 30 year high—with the Rocky Mountain Region having the highest rates in the country!

A new study from the Washington University School of Medicine in St. Louis, Missouri, found that people who smoke marijuana before age 17 are 3.5 times more likely to attempt suicide as those who started smoking marijuana later in life. In addition, the study found that people who are dependent on marijuana have a higher risk of experiencing major depression and suicidal thoughts and behaviors.

A New Zealand Study found that not only did the cannabis use precipitate suicidal thoughts, but also that the higher the frequency of regular use the faster susceptible individuals became suicidal. The study was based on data gathered from 1,265 children born in 1977 who were studied at birth, at four months, one year, and then at annual intervals to the age of 16, and after that at the ages of 18, 21, 25 and 30. Information on cannabis habits and suicidal feelings was by self-report. The authors stated "Our results indicate that the earlier that intense use (at least several times per week) first occurs, the faster susceptible individuals start having suicidal thoughts."

The impact of cannabis on suicidal thoughts was quantified in a model contained in the study, which found, if all males used cannabis less frequently than several times per week, suicidal ideation would be experienced by 15 per cent of 18 year olds, 24 per cent of 21 year olds and by 30 per cent of 30 year olds. By contrast, if they all started using cannabis several times a week from the age of 17 then the population prevalence of suicidal ideation for males would increase to 24 per cent for 18 year olds, and 31 per cent for 21 year olds.

In an International Study, heavy cannabis use was associated with a four-fold increase in completed suicide in a 15-year follow-up of 45,540 Swedish conscripts. Medically serious suicide attempters were found to be ten times more likely to be regular cannabis users than general population controls in a New Zealand sample.

Conservatively, a valid interpretation of the research clearly indicates strong likelihood that marijuana use exacerbates depression where it pre-exists and causes depression for those who may use it frequently and/or over a long period of time. For many, the end result of lengthy and serious depression is suicidal ideation, and for many the suicidal thoughts end as suicide itself. Depression is a very dark and painful place. The caution is to not start down that path via marijuana.

# FETAL MARIJUANA EFFECTS AND MARIJUANA RELATED BIRTH DEFECTS

THC (delta-9-hydrocannabinol), the psychoactive ingredient in marijuana, is known to pass from the mother to the developing fetus through the placenta. This means that the fetus is affected by any amount of marijuana taken by the pregnant woman, placing it at a greater risk of complications. The effect of marijuana on a fetus may not be fully quantified, but in either situation marijuana should be totally avoided. For instance, any form of smoking can disrupt the supply of oxygen and nutrients to the fetus which can result in restrictions in the growth of the fetus (including overall length, foot length, head size and body weight), and in rare cases can cause premature birth, miscarriage and stillbirth.

According to information provided through the University of Washington, there is some evidence that women who use marijuana during pregnancy are more likely to give birth to babies with lower birth weight, delayed commencement of breathing, an increase in features similar to those found in fetal alcohol syndrome, exaggerated startle response, tremors, poorer eye-sight, poorer ability to adapt to new aspects of the environment, and a "hole in the heart" (ventricular septal defect).

Other studies have found that in the first six months of life, babies who have been exposed to marijuana in utero are also at greater risk of developing asthma, chest infections, and other breathing problems such as wheezing.

Research suggests that, at ages three-to-four years, children of mothers who used marijuana while pregnant have poorer verbal, memory and reasoning ability; poorer motor skills and shorter length of play; and are more likely to be fearful, impulsive, inattentive, hyperactive and delinquent. These difficulties appear to persist to age 10 years, when they may be accompanied by increased depression and anxiety, along with reading and spelling problems and general underachievement at school. Such deficits may also continue into adolescence and early adulthood, along with an increased risk for initiation of tobacco and marijuana use.

In addition, there exists some evidence that mothers' marijuana use during pregnancy increases the risk of their children developing childhood cancers, including non-lymphoblastic leukemia, rhabdomyosarcoma (a rare, highly malignant tumor that can occur anywhere in the body), and astrocytoma (a type of brain tumor.)

Preliminary research suggests that fathers' marijuana use in the year prior to their children's birth is associated with an increased risk of rhabdomyosarcoma in their children, and that fathers' marijuana use during conception, pregnancy or postnatally is associated with an increased risk of Sudden Infant Death Syndrome (SIDS) in their infants. Furthermore, some research suggests that children of fathers who experience marijuana dependence at least at some point in their lifetimes are more likely to experience negative outcomes during childhood, such as poor attachment relationships with their caregivers and psychosocial impairments, including depression and conduct problems.

Studies show that marijuana may seriously affect fetal development. Lower birth weights, a shorter gestation period, major malformations, and the occurrence of miscarriages increase with marijuana use by pregnant women. There is a risk of harm after birth for breast-feeding infants if their mothers use marijuana as it passes through breast milk in almost pure form to the infant. Even prior to conception, marijuana use causes changes in both males and females. It causes a decrease in testosterone, the production of fewer sperm, and the production of sperm with more abnormal chromosomes for the fathers-to-be. In addition marijuana may produce more testosterone and tends to produce less healthy eggs in females. With poorer quality eggs and sperm with abnormal defects, there is an increased occurrence of birth defects.

Marijuana also interferes with cell division, a process crucial for reproduction for healthy fetal growth and development. One laboratory study of pregnant rats exposed to cannabis produced less fertile offspring with smaller reproductive organs, and another study demonstrated that embryonic development may be halted before the three-day stage suggesting that embryos are prevented from attaching to the uterine wall if exposed to marijuana.

While studies demonstrate mixed findings, moderate marijuana use was found to be related to increased risk of ocular hypertelorism and epicanthus; and other studies have suggested that there may be significant (although temporary) differences in the behavior patterns and nervous systems of infants whose mothers frequently used marijuana during pregnancy. Preliminary findings from a 15 year study indicate that prenatal exposure to marijuana impairs decision making, future planning, cognition (reasoning and memory) and sustained attention among children who were marijuana-exposed babies.

In a study published in the Journal of the American Academy of Child and Adolescent Psychiatry, it was reported that 7,452 mothers were enrolled during pregnancy and the developing fetus was monitored for fetal growth during early, middle and late stage pregnancy. The study found that maternal cannabis use during pregnancy was associated "with growth restriction in mid-and-late term pregnancy, and with lower birth weight. This growth reduction was most pronounced for fetuses exposed to continued maternal cannabis use during pregnancy, compared with non-exposed fetuses. Maternal cannabis use during pregnancy resulted in more pronounced growth restriction than maternal tobacco use. The study concluded that maternal cannabis use, even for a short period, may be associated with several adverse fetal growth trajectories.

Research has more clearly defined the types of complications and health problems that fetal exposure to marijuana may include—again even including miscarriages. Every woman wants a healthy baby. Every baby deserves a chance to be born healthy—and drug free.

# MARIJUANA AND VIOLENCE

Although cannabis is generally perceived as an "innocuous" drug, research has soundly proven that marijuana may cause mental illness, intensify mental illness, or exacerbate mental illness in those with a pre-disposition or genetic vulnerability—even to the point of causing a full psychotic break.

There is now sound evidence that taking cannabis leads to acute adverse mental effects in a high proportion of regular users. Many of these effects are dose-related, but adverse symptoms may be aggravated by constitutional factors including youthfulness, personality attributes, and vulnerability to serious mental illness.

Marijuana has different effects on different people. Anger, rage, aggression and violence may be one set of those effects, depending upon the user, the drug, the dosage and frequency of use, and the set and setting of use.

One woman who lives with her husband and family noticed that when he is using marijuana he gets extremely angry very easily and cannot control his anger impulses. His aggression builds and he yells a lot—even in front of their children, uses profane language, sometimes throws or breaks things, and also shoves or grabs her or spits on her. She sees that his whole personality changes when he smokes and in the 10 years with him as soon as he quits smoking his personality goes back to normal and the anger and aggression stop. Like so many family members, this woman was questioning her own sanity instead of fully acknowledging that it was the marijuana.

One man refused to see that when he smoked pot he was like Dr. Jekyll turning into Mr. Hyde. According to his wife, he claimed to smoke just to relax, but the result was that he "would go from nice to psycho." She saw what years of marijuana dependence could do. But she also saw that after quitting for at least one month her husband would return the nicest husband ever. But then when he starts again, so does the screaming and calling of names and abuse. She advises that before anyone begins to use marijuana they spend a week in her house and see what pot really does. In this case the reality of marijuana is that it is going to cost this man his family.

Another woman who smoked pot day and night for years, did so to "relax and chill," or so she thought. When she wasn't stoned, she later realized, she got angry and overreacted to "stupid things." By nature she was not an aggressive person at all, so it wasn't that. And when she quit pot two years ago she stopped getting angry and overreacting to things. Today she is much calmer and much happier, and glad she quit. She also admits that for the years that she smoked it, she would be adamant that she wasn't addicted and she thought pot actually made her calmer and not angry or aggressive at all. It took quitting marijuana to make her see just what the real effects of it on her were and that in fact the total opposite of what she had believed was true. Not only that, but it made her so lazy, she lost track of all her hopes and dreams. Now that she has quit, she has sorted her life out, has traveled, and has entered into a professional career course of study.

Another woman admitted to smoking pot for every day for eight years. The only time she didn't have any marijuana was when she couldn't get any which wasn't often. She became such an angry person that little things would set her off like a cashier taking too long at a shop, or someone getting in her way. She got to the point where she just became a habitually angry person, and would and did shout and say the most abusive things to people and make a spectacle of herself in front of others. She felt generalized anger towards most people, lost all feeling of trust in people, and began thinking everyone had a hidden agenda. Her paranoia built until she managed to push away every friend she ever had. This woman lost all friends until her only friend was her dog, and she even began to mistreat the dog in bursts of fury over stupid things. Of course later she would have guilt and remorse for the way she treated people and her dog. Her anger also got her into trouble with the police as well. She couldn't control it and knew that she did not want to live like that because she was, in fact, a good person. She just needed to find out the hard way that it was the marijuana smoking that changed her personality and turned her into the angry person she never thought she would become.

One young man who used to be a heavy pot smoker, now admits that "weed has the worst effect on your mind." He also found out the hard way that it is not the social drug that people think it is and it is very hard to quit. He now admits that he lost his best friends because of weed and he lost the girl that he loved so much, because the marijuana disturbed his mind and altered his moods. He got so addicted to marijuana that he couldn't control his anger, and he became mean to his friends and was so mean to his girlfriend that after a year of being together she got a restraining order because she became scared of him. Like so many others who have come to this realization, after quitting he saw the damage he never realized it was doing and now he hopes that kids do not start smoking marijuana. He now openly admits that weed is highly addictive and it "messes with your head," until you get to the point that you are not going to know who you are and how to live without smoking weed. He cautions, "please don't start or if you have, please stop."

Today researchers have noted seven distinct areas of marijuana "induced" aggression and violence: First, while one is experiencing marijuana withdrawal, there is a greater tendency toward aggression as a symptom of working through the withdrawal process itself. Second, when marijuana users also drink alcohol it can result in a synergistic effect intensified with the marijuana which enhances emotional affect and increases tendencies toward violence. The point here is that most marijuana smokers also drink alcohol, thus, naturally increasing the possibility/probability of anger, rage, aggression and violence. Third, research also shows that cannabis users who have a history of violence before marijuana use may be more likely to commit aggressive acts after they start using the drug. Perhaps too, sociopathy and psychopathology as preexisting personality traits can be exacerbated by marijuana use. Fourth, there is some belief that young smokers who experience extreme paranoia, anxiety and fear could lead to aggressive outbursts when under the influence. This tends to happen more in young smokers who have other issues factoring in to their aggressive behavior. In these younger users, the cannabis can actually promote an aggressive response if there are other emotional low points or issues in the person's life and the cannabis exacerbates those underlying issues. Fifth, many studies have noted the increased rebelliousness in youth after beginning marijuana use, and some also note a further development into a type of aggressiveness.

Marijuana use may stunt emotional maturation, and one misses the developmental sequence of coping skills with marijuana use in those formative years. Sixth, studies show that violence can occur more often among people who use cannabis regularly, rather than those who use it occasionally or not at all, thus, frequency of use is a factor lending toward marijuana related violence. Seventh, research shows that the expectations and characteristics of the users itself may exacerbate violence while under the influence of marijuana, i.e., members of a violence prone gang may be more likely to act out violently when high.

These seven areas are documented by researchers, but certainly there can be other reasons or instances in which marijuana use precipitates anger, aggressiveness or violence.

One study on a college campus found that either the use of alcohol or a combination of alcohol use and marijuana use were more common to violence on the college campus. The study found that substance use may be involved in as much as forty-four percent of the violence and that in the event of a conflict instead of turning away substance users might tend to aggravate the situation or adopt more of a confrontational/aggressive stance.

The National Research Council has concluded that the "long-term use of marijuana may alter the nervous system in ways that do promote violence." One example of this may actually be Amsterdam. The myth of the Netherlands as a well-functioning society with their loose drug policy is false. Amsterdam is one of Europe's most violent cities. In fact Amsterdam is in the process of closing marijuana dispensaries because of the crime associated with their operation (they are also concerned with the use among young people and the social consequences, which range from poor school performance and truancy to serious impairment, including brain damage.) As an aside, the myth that the possible cause of the delinquency and aggression problems were due to the users coming into contact with the illegal black market and drug dealers has now been discounted.

In Los Angeles, police report that areas surrounding cannabis clubs have experienced a 200 percent increase in robberies, a 52.2 percent increase in burglaries, a 57.1 percent increase in aggravated assault, and a 130.8 percent increase in burglaries from automobiles.

A spokesperson for Europe Against Drugs, said their findings backed research showing a link between cannabis and violent offenses, such as assault. They noted that *"Cannabis is by far the most common drug involved. Many people will be surprised by the number of cannabis users who have been arrested for these crimes."*

Another research paper in 2002 found cannabis implicated in violence. It found that alcohol dependent individuals were almost twice as likely to be violent, but cannabis dependents almost four times more likely to be violent than controls (people who did not abuse the substances).

In a study of youth published in 2013 in the Journal of Studies on Alcohol and Drugs, it was stated that there is extensive overlap of victimization and aggression in both peer and dating relationships, and those with high rates of violence across relationships have increased alcohol and marijuana use. The findings concluded that violence prevention efforts should consider addressing concomitant substance use.

In several youth self-reported surveys, the researchers found that frequent marijuana users were more likely than less frequent users to report delinquent behaviors and aggressive behaviors such as destroying things that belong to others and physically attacking people. Users were two-to-four times more likely than non-users to report they think about killing themselves or that they deliberately try to hurt or kill themselves. They were more likely than non-users to say they were unhappy, sad or depressed and that they feel "no one loves me." The users were more likely than nonusers to report that "others are out to get me" and "I am suspicious". One interesting fact is that drug use by persons with antisocial personality could reasonably be expected to increase any tendency to act violently. Thus, if there is a pre-existing or underlying sociopathy issue, marijuana use could exacerbate these latent tendencies toward aggression or violence.

One particular European article identified a strain of marijuana that seemed to fill youths with a "lawless bravado" which "turns them into criminals and even potential killers." The commentator was concerned that it transformed users into dangerous "schizophrenics", and when they use this brand of cannabis there is an altered state of mind that can lead to murder. This concern addressed the murder of a father of two who requested that the marijuana users make less noise as he had to get up and go to work early the next morning. They killed him.

Researchers are now discovering the relationship between road rage and marijuana use. One study surveyed 2500 people to examine the relationship between alcohol and marijuana use and the incidence of road rage. The data was very revealing. Of those participants who identified themselves as drivers, 5% had engaged in road rage behavior, 15% had experienced a road rage incident and 24% had both experienced and perpetrated a road rage incident. The risk for perpetrating road rage was directly linked to previous year DUI with alcohol or marijuana involved. The risk for serious road rage while driving DUI drove the risks even higher…even passengers were more likely to experience and engage in road rage if the driver of their car was using alcohol or marijuana or both.

It is very interesting that many articles begin by explaining that marijuana usually has a sedating effect on most users, making it much less likely to cause violence in users than other substances such as alcohol and stimulants. These articles then go on to dismiss the findings of marijuana use with aggression, abuse or violence, and attempt to minimize them and explain them away by blaming them on other psychological and sociological factors. In this case psychological or sociological factors really do not matter. If a person does not speed he does not break the law. If he is drunk and speeds he breaks the law no matter what the underlying factors are. The same is true for marijuana. If a person does not speed he does not break the law. If he speeds because he is under the influence of marijuana then he breaks the law. It is not all the other personality, psychological or sociological factors—it is the direct influence of the drug marijuana.

Using cannabis can produce strange behaviors and reactions in people when they are intoxicated. These reactions can be fueled by confusion, feeling threatened or frightened, or even feelings of paranoia or persecution. As marijuana chemically affects the brain and neurotransmitters, as it alters mood regulators, as it interferes with the cognitive functions, and as it developmentally delays emotional maturation many people will feel anger and rage, and aggression and violence will be an unexpected and unwanted resultant issue.

Seeing that there is evidence that marijuana use can lead to aggressiveness, anger and perhaps rage, the question remains can marijuana lead to actual violence or exacerbate violent tendencies in those with a predisposition to violence?

The answer, clearly, is yes.

Chaos—including murder, torture, and home made terrorism—has happened, is happening, and will only increase with easier accessibility of marijuana. This is a strong statement, but the fact remains that marijuana does four things: it clouds emotions, it impairs cognitive functioning, it increases sensitivity to stimuli and accentuates different streams of consciousness, and it can certainly exacerbate mental illness. Alone or together, the effects of marijuana are correlated with violence and a range of violent acts.

There is now sound evidence that taking cannabis leads to acute adverse mental effects in a high proportion of regular users. Marijuana exacerbates mental illness. It may increase paranoia, cause delusions of persecution, delusions of grandeur, suspiciousness, and even psychosis or sociopathy. Cannabis misuse makes a significant contribution to self-harm, contributes to adjustment disorder with depressed mood, major depression, and dysthymia. Paranoia and acute anxiety are common features, as are feelings of detachment, depersonalization, derealization, a feeling of loss of control, fear of dying, irrational panic and paranoid ideas, psychotic symptoms, and conspiracy or risk of harm from others. Cannabis use may precipitate a toxic psychosis with symptoms of confusion and hallucination, an acute functional psychosis similar to an acute schizophreniform state, a chronic psychosis which persists after abstinence, an organic psychosis which only partially remits after abstinence, and cannabis use may be a risk-factor for other serious mental illnesses such as schizophrenia.

Thus, it is not a far reach to say that if marijuana exacerbates certain types of mental illness, it can logically be said to also precipitate violent acts.

As a historical example, the Assassins (more properly known as the Hashhashin) belonged to a mystical Sufi Muslim sect and smoked hashish. They were best known for their dramatic executions of political figures. So well known were the Assassins that maps during the Crusades marked the Syrian coast as the "Country of the Assassins." Their name comes from the Arabic hashishiyya. The English word "assassin" was derived from "hashishin," which means "taker of hashish." The drug's powers were thought to explain the Assassins' bravery and savagery.

Lore holds that they would smoke hashish before going into battle. Some regard them as being the first terrorists and sowing the seeds of terrorist thought and tactics in the Islamic world. They called themselves fidayeen ("martyrs"), and they would carry out any command, even brutally killing themselves. The savagery and ferocity of their violence was feared by all.

So is it possible that today, marijuana impairs judgment, and causes violence including murder and even terrorism? The answer is yes.

The Boston Marathon Bombers, the brothers Tsarnaev (Tamerlan and Dzhokhar Tsarnaev) were confirmed marijuana smokers.

The "Vampire Rapist", John Crutchley, found guilty of kidnapping, sexual battery, and who drained and drank the blood of his victims, and was suspected of multiple murders, was a marijuana smoker.

Thomas Palmer, a habitual cannabis user, murdered two school friends with a hunting knife in an "explosion of anger" which left one of them with his head almost severed. Philip Joseph, an expert witness for the prosecution, said that any psychotic symptoms "were likely to have been caused by heavy cannabis use."

A heavy user of powerful "skunk" cannabis, Ezekiel Maxwell was 17 when he launched a frenzied attack on Carmelita Tulloch, a 51 year-old grandmother, killing her in a savage and brutal way and without mercy. Psychiatric reports stated that at the time of the stabbing, he was suffering from paranoid schizophrenia which was exacerbated by heavy use of "skunk".

Rudy Eugene—the Florida man who was suspected to be high on "bath salts" when he was shot and killed by police after refusing to stop chewing a homeless man's face—was not on "bath salts" after all. According to the Miami-Dade County medical examiner's office, toxicology tests performed on Eugene found marijuana in his system, but no street drugs, prescription drugs or alcohol.

Ariel Castro, the man accused of kidnapping, rape, torture, and of holding 3 girls for a decade in his home in Cleveland, was allegedly a marijuana smoker.

James Holmes, 24, the "Batman—the Dark Knight" cinema rampage killer in Aurora, Colorado, was allegedly a marijuana smoker.

Jared Lee Loughner, the Arizona Shooter of Congresswoman Gabrielle Giffords was allegedly a marijuana smoker.

Gerald Patrick Lewis, who murdered six women across Alabama, Georgia, and Massachusetts, was allegedly a marijuana smoker.

Adam Lanza, the Connecticut child killer who fatally shot 20 children and 6 adult staff members in a mass murder at

Sandy Hook Elementary School in Newtown, Connecticut, was allegedly a marijuana smoker.

Phillip Marshall, who killed his teen children Alex and Macaila in their sleep in Florida and then committed suicide, allegedly "was smoking a lot of (marijuana)."

Richard Ramierez, the "Night Stalker" serial killer of Los Angeles was according to his father, "a good boy…until his marijuana use sent him out of control."

John Wayne Gacy, the "Killer Clown" serial killer and rapist of at least 22 victims, was a confirmed marijuana smoker.

"The Milwaukee Cannibal": Jeffrey Lionel Dahmer was found guilty of being a serial killer, rape, dismemberment, necrophilia, cannibalism, and a killer of 17 victims over a 13 year period, was a marijuana smoker.

Columbine Massacre: There is some evidence that Eric Harris, 18, one of the two shooters at the Columbine High School massacre that left 15 dead and 28 hurt had smoked marijuana. Allegedly, Eric had said that what he does on the weekends "is set off pipe bombs & get stoned." Dylan Klebold, age 17, claimed he had only "tried it twice and didn't like it."

Pentagon Shooter: Pentagon shooter John Patrick Bedell was a "psychotic pothead" who believed government was standing in the way of his desire to use, grow and glorify marijuana. He virtually worshipped the drug. "I'm a cannabis enthusiast." In 2012, he shot and wounded 2 Pentagon Police Officers. Bedell holds a medical marijuana card for "health reasons."

The Red Lake High School Massacre: Jeffrey James Weise who killed his grandfather and 8 school victims (one teacher and students), then committed suicide later the same day, described himself as "nothin' but your average Native American stoner" and "MJ is my gal of choice."

Robert Andrew “Bob” Berdella a serial killer in Kansas City, who raped, tortured and killed at least six men, was arrested for possession of marijuana.

Herbert William Mullin, a serial killer who committed 13 murders in California in the early 1970s, was allegedly a marijuana smoker.

Russell Ellwood who was arrested in connection to two murders, but suspected in as many as 24(+) killings, was a marijuana smoker.

Mass murderer George Jo Hennard, who killed 23 victims by shooting in Killeen, Texas, was allegedly a marijuana smoker.

Sean Vincent Gillis, who killed 8 women ages 30-82, by stabbing or by strangulation, in Baton Rouge Louisiana, was allegedly a marijuana smoker.

Kyle Aaron Huff, who killed six victims in the Capital Hill neighborhood of Seattle Washington then committed suicide when confronted by the police, was allegedly a marijuana smoker.

Wesley Neal Higdon, who shot and killed his supervisor and 4 co-workers and critically injured a sixth victim, then committed suicide, in Henderson, Kentucky, was allegedly a marijuana smoker.

Mitchell Scott Johnson, one of the two shooters in the Westside Middle School Massacre school shooting that occurred in Craighead County, Arkansas where a total of 5 people (four female students and a teacher) were killed and 10 people were injured, was allegedly a marijuana smoker.

Leonard Lake, who raped, tortured and killed up to 25 victims throughout California, and committed suicide when arrested, was allegedly a marijuana smoker.

Clifton McCree had marijuana in his system when he gunned down five people and then killed himself in Fort Lauderdale, FL., and toxicology tests revealed no sign of any stronger drugs or alcohol.

Ricardo Muñoz Ramirez, guilty of rape, robberies, and mutilation and murder of some 16+ victims, in Los Angeles, said, smoking marijuana "was one of only three things" he was interested in.

Eddie Lee Mosley, found guilty of rape and strangulation of up to 16 people in Fort Lauderdale, FL., was allegedly a marijuana smoker.

Brian Gene Nichols found guilty of murder of 4 victims and accused and convicted of 54 crimes, was allegedly a marijuana smoker.

Itzcoatl Ocampo, a serial killer of 6 victims in Orange County, CA., had a "Medical Marijuana" license.

The Stockton Massacre: Patrick Edward Purdy, a convicted murderer of 5 victims (school children ages 5-9), in Stockton, CA., was allegedly a marijuana smoker.

Larry Ralston, a rapist and murderer of 5 victims in Ohio, was allegedly a marijuana smoker.

The "Coast-to-Coast" Killer: Tommy Lynn Sells, suspected of murdering up to 13 victims across the country, allegedly began smoking marijuana at 10 years old.

Spree Killer Nicholas Troy Sheley, of Rock Falls, Illinois, allegedly committed eight murders by blunt force trauma to the head—including a 2 year old child, had been arrested frequently since adolescence for crimes including marijuana possession.

John Sapp who killed four victims by shooting (including his mother), allegedly was a marijuana smoker.

Joseph Edward Duncan III found guilty of rape, kidnapping, and a serial killer of up to 7 victims by hitting them with a hammer, was allegedly a marijuana smoker.

Banita Jacks killed her four daughters who "were possessed by demons" by strangulation and stabbing. She smoked marijuana and allowed their "3 and 4 year old daughters to smoke" while (they) sat and laughed.

Aileen Carol Pittman who said, "I've hated humans for a very long time" and who murdered seven(+) men in Florida, was allegedly a marijuana smoker.

Francesco Acevedo guilty of rape and murder of three women in Yonkers and who had a long history of violence, sexual assault, larceny, assault, harassment and drunken driving, began using marijuana (and alcohol and other drugs) at age 12.

Charles Andy Williams, age 15, was allegedly a regular marijuana user who smoked the drug just before killing two schoolmates and wounding 13 others in a San Diego suburban school.

Kinman Chan, 30, fought with crew members of US Airways Flight 1447. He made odd gestures, disrupted the cross-country flight, dropped his Pants, attacked the crew, and began to scream. He nearly caused an airline disaster. Chan told agents that he has a medical marijuana card and ate double his normal dose of marijuana cookies while waiting for his flight to depart.

Mother's Day Parade Shooters: Brothers Akein (age 19) and Shawn (age 24) Scott, who were arrested and charged with 20 counts of second degree attempted murder at the shootings at the 2013 Mother's Day Parade in New Orleans, were allegedly marijuana smokers.

Osama bin Laden: Nic Robertson, a journalist from CNN, found a cannabis crop alongside a garden of cabbages and potatoes at Abbottabad, Osama bin Laden's top-secret compound. (But whether or not bin Laden and his family were growing marijuana for recreational purposes, medical purposes or spiritual purposes remains a mystery.)

In addition to its short-term effects on sensory perception, marijuana use can impair decision-making and self-control during and long after intoxication. While good judgment and self-control improves from youth into adulthood with maturity, it tends to degenerate with substance abuse and dependence. Teens who use marijuana are more likely to engage in delinquent and dangerous behavior. Self-control inhibits risk-seeking and impulsive behaviors that limit educational attainment and contribute to criminal conduct, and researchers have studied and documented these effects. According to one study, *"the probability of being arrested for a non-drug involved violent, property and income-producing crime" is greater for marijuana users than non-users.*

In California, where "medical" marijuana has been sold since 2003, marijuana dispensary neighborhoods have attracted criminal acts of violence such as armed robbery, murder, and even increasingly organized crime involvement.

According to the Arrestee Drug Abuse Monitoring Program (ADAM II), marijuana remained the drug most often detected in arrestees in all five sites in 2012, ranging from 37 percent in Atlanta to 58 percent in Chicago. In three of the five sites, over half of the adult male arrestees for violent crime, property crime, drug-related crimes, income producing crimes or other crimes tested positive for marijuana.

In a release from the Youth Justice Board in the United Kingdom, they found that more than seven out of ten teenage criminals have smoked cannabis every day for at least twelve months. The study shows a shocking link between use of the drug and a youth's chances of ending up behind bars. The report said that of the 6,500 individuals who pass through young offender institutions every year, 72 per cent have used cannabis "daily" in the year leading to arrest. It was speculated that marijuana use causes youth to stop caring about committing crimes, and that this study reinforces the link between cannabis and crime.

According to the FBI's Uniform Crime Reporting Data, there were a total of 1.5 million drug arrests made nationwide in 2011, and out of those arrests, about 750,000 were for marijuana (just under half, 49.5 percent). What the crime statistics do not tell you is the number of those arrests which are actually marijuana related crime events associated with marijuana possession, i.e., theft, larceny, D.U.I., murder and non-negligent manslaughter, forcible rape, robbery, aggravated assault, burglary, motor vehicle theft, arson, domestic violence, child abuse and neglect, etc.

A common myth being circulated is that these marijuana arrests are for "simple possession." In truth, the vast majority are either directly related to such crime(s) or otherwise discovered during an investigation where other probable cause and or criminal activity has been defined and marijuana may be complicit in the overall (criminal) lifestyle or behavior(s). In fact, under current laws few offenders are in prison for simple marijuana possession. No more than two-tenths of one percent (0.2%) of federal inmates are locked up for marijuana possession, and among state prisoners only one-tenth of one percent (0.1%) are in for marijuana possession without a prior record. Predictably, most of these prisoners are charged with probation or parole violations or with possession of wholesale quantities where intent to distribute could not be proved.

Certainly a number of studies have concluded that there is no relationship between marijuana use and aggression, and certainly studies on college campuses and among certain groups show that marijuana is less conducive to violence than alcohol.

Although the marijuana-aggressiveness relationship has not been a proven constant, i.e., for 100 percent of marijuana users, it certainly warrants significant concern and a continued warning that marijuana related aggression, anger, rage and violence is real and can be a significant side effect of marijuana use.

# YOUTH SELF-REPORTS

With drug use, researchers and clinicians can often find the most compelling evidence of impact from the testimonies of users and former users.

In the report, "Adolescent Self-Reported Behaviors and Their Association with Marijuana Use" (*Janet C. Greenblatt, June 03, 2008, Source: Office of Applied Studies, SAMHSA, National Household Survey on Drug Abuse),* several important findings were noted regarding marijuana related problems—*as reported by youth themselves*.

*Social Problems*: Those who used marijuana in the past year were more likely than nonusers to not get along with other youth, and weekly users were nearly twice as likely as nonusers to report this.

*Thought Problems*: Past year marijuana users age 12-to-17 were more likely than nonusers to report thought problems like "I can not get my mind off certain thoughts", or "I repeat certain actions over and over." In addition, frequent users were more likely to see or hear things that other people think are not there.

*Attention Problems*: Those who used marijuana in the past year were more likely than nonusers to report they have trouble concentrating, are confused or in a fog, daydream a lot, or act without stopping to think.

*Delinquent Behavior*: The greatest differences between users and nonusers were found in measures of delinquent behavior. Frequent users were 6 times as likely to run away from home; nearly 6 times as likely to say they had cut classes or skipped school; and 3-to-5 times as likely to steal, report they do not feel guilty after doing something they should not, hang around with kids who get into trouble, and lie and cheat. All problem areas increased in frequency as the marijuana use increased.

This one study, then, points out that there are severe and long lasting effects of marijuana use, as reported by youth themselves.

In another study by the National Household Survey on Drug Abuse (NHSDA), it was reported that among those children and teens (12-to-17 year-olds) using marijuana on 12 or more days during the past year nearly 75% experienced significant problems related to use, and 42 percent experienced three or more problems including loss of control over their use.

# MARIJUANA WITHDRAWAL SYNDROME

One of the greatest myths about marijuana is that it is not addictive. But long-term marijuana use can most certainly lead to marijuana dependency, and yes, addiction. According to the World Health Organization, the symptoms of marijuana dependence include increased tolerance, loss of control over predictable use, long term inability to cut down or stop use, pre-occupation with obtaining or use of the drug, and less time devoted to family, school, work and recreation. Dr. Chris Thurstone, an adolescent psychiatrist who runs a substance abuse treatment program at Denver Health and a recognized authority on chemical dependency stated, "We need to tell people that youth are the most likely to become addicted to marijuana and that when they become addicted, they are at higher risk for every bad outcome a teenager can face. There is no debate in the scientific community," Thurstone said, "it's physically and mentally addictive."

For many years, addiction professionals have seen a noticeable syndrome developing with users who suddenly stop smoking marijuana. A withdrawal syndrome is a hallmark feature that occurs with the cessation of use of addictive drugs. It is a result of cellular adaptation and a progression of tolerance. It can be an uncomfortable and even painful experience that results from stopping the use of a drug that was taken over a period of time.

Most people are familiar with addiction and withdrawal from nicotine, and while that is a strong addiction that results in a strong craving for continued use, the fact is that nicotine itself is one of the weaker drugs of addiction and does not present the plethora of issues that withdrawal from other drugs do.

Evidence is accumulating that a cannabis withdrawal syndrome is common, of clinical significance, and has a clear time course. This is supported both by clinical evidence as well as the reports by users themselves.

Of course not all marijuana users experience withdrawal when they try to quit. Furthermore, one person's experience of cannabis withdrawal might be quite different from another's, and the severity depends on a host of factors including the potency of the drug, the frequency of use, and the length of use. But many do present withdrawal symptoms with an associated discomfort, and may even need treatment and support to help maintain their abstinence until they work through the withdrawal process.

For marijuana withdrawal, the most common symptom is sleep disturbance, including insomnia which can last from a few nights of practically no sleep at all up to a few months of broken and/or occasional sleeplessness. Nightmares and vivid dreams are frequent, and the dreams can be with vivid colors, strong emotions or nightmares. These can last about a month and then taper off. Dreams or nightmares may even be about using marijuana, and these dreams can last perhaps for years after someone has quit use. About 50 percent of marijuana users report sleep disturbances when quitting.

The next set of common symptoms are depression and irritability, anger or even rage and aggression. Here this can include either a "constant" irritability or even sudden bursts of anger when least expected. Emotional lability and mood swings are very common with emotions bouncing back and forth between depression, anger, and euphoria. Sometimes one feels fear or anxiety, seems to lose their sense of humor, or sees a change in their sex drive. This emotional lability tends to fade and returns back to normal usually within a three month period. During withdrawal, one may also see a loss of concentration or disruption of usual cognitive functions for the first few weeks.

Headaches may be another common feature of withdrawal, more intense at first and perhaps lasting a few weeks after quitting. Many reported night sweats. Some report eating problems, including loss of appetite, digestion problems or nausea. Again, these tend to fade after a period of a few weeks. Some who quit reported more severe symptoms such as tremors or shaking and dizziness, and intense discomfort.

Craving for marijuana, the intense desire to continue to use, is the most commonly reported withdrawal syndrome. One study reported that 75.7 percent of participants trying to quit experienced intense cravings for marijuana. Some other symptoms reported—although not as frequent, include kidney pain, impotency, hormone changes or imbalances, chronic fatigue, eye problems, etc. These tend to resolve themselves after several weeks.

People can experience very real withdrawal symptoms when they quit marijuana that can affect their daily lives. A new study from Australia studied habitual marijuana users who had quit for two weeks. As per the study at the National Cannabis Prevention and Information Centre at the University of New South Wales, they reported experiencing irritability, sleep difficulties and other symptoms that affected their ability to work and their relationships with other people. The greatest impairments were seen among users who were the most addicted to marijuana. The withdrawal symptoms that contributed most to impairment were physical tension, sleep problems, anxiety, depression, mood swings, loss of appetite, and craving. In fact these were so pronounced, that 20 percent of the group in the study relapsed back into marijuana use during the study itself.

Typically withdrawal syndrome presents with symptoms that appear to be the exact opposite of an abused drug's direct effects. The National Epidemiologic Survey on Alcohol and Related Conditions examined a group of over 1,100 regular marijuana users who didn't binge drink or regularly use other drugs or narcotics. The respondents in the survey pointed to a marked set of symptoms that were experienced when they suddenly stopped the consumption of marijuana, and the symptoms immediately resolved when marijuana use was restarted. Those who responded to the survey reported three or more symptoms of cannabis withdrawal syndrome. Two types of withdrawal symptoms emerged in the survey, somatic and psychological. Somatic related symptoms included weakness, psychomotor retardation and sleep disturbances. Psychological symptoms included depression, hyper-anxiety and panic disorder. Respondents who experienced personality disorders concurrent to the use of cannabis, found that the underlying personality problem was exacerbated and more pronounced upon withdrawal from marijuana.

A Duke University study of 496 adult marijuana smokers who tried to quit found that 95.5% of them experienced at least one withdrawal symptom while 43.1% experienced more than one symptom. The number of symptoms the participants experienced was significantly linked to how often and how much the subjects smoked prior to trying to quit. Those who were daily smokers experienced the most symptoms, but even those who reported using marijuana less than weekly experienced some withdrawal symptoms of moderate intensity.

Researchers say that heavy pot users who quit cold turkey begin smoking again to alleviate withdrawal symptoms. In one study of nearly 500 marijuana smokers who tried to quit, about one-third failed and began to use again to deal with withdrawal symptoms such as irritability and anxiety. "There's long been a debate over whether pot smokers actually become addicted to the drug and whether withdrawal symptoms are real. They do and they are", said researcher David Gorelick, MD, PhD, of the National Institute on Drug Abuse in Baltimore. In the study, a total of 42.4% of the heavy smokers experienced at least one withdrawal symptom—most commonly, cravings, irritability, boredom, anxiety, and sleep disturbances when they tried to quit. Overall, 33.3% of participants resumed cannabis use to reduce or avoid withdrawal symptoms.

As research shows that cannabis withdrawal can and does occur when heavy marijuana users quit, now Cannabis Withdrawal has been included in the Diagnostic and Statistical Manual of Mental Disorders (DSM-5.) Doctors and psychiatrists have found that although cannabis withdrawal lasts anywhere from a few days to a week or more, some marijuana users experience several weeks or months of withdrawal symptoms, known as post acute withdrawal syndrome (PAWS). Findings also show that chronic use can precipitate substance-induced anxiety disorders.

Marijuana is no laughing matter, and should be considered serious by all. Again, marijuana, like alcohol and all street drugs, is a drug of dependency. The withdrawal syndrome proves it.

# MARIJUANA AND DUI

Driving while intoxicated, more commonly referred to as driving while under the influence when it involves drug intoxication, is an epidemic in the United States that has cost many millions of lives and countless hundreds of millions of dollars in human and social costs such as insurance, health care and criminal justice costs. In addition, the degree of needless human suffering and misery can never be adequately described, measured, or understood by the victims who tragically suffer from these accidents.

In terms of driving while intoxicated with marijuana, marijuana use impairs driving-related functions and there is a definite increased risk for auto accidents. It impairs motor coordination, alters sense of time and distance, and makes one drowsy. One study demonstrated severe balance impairment and two-and-one-half times more errors in coordination tests in a dose-response fashion.

First, it needs to be noted that driving while intoxicated under the influence of alcohol has dropped significantly over these years. Yes, more than a million people are injured each year due to alcohol related traffic accidents, but overall, nationally alcohol related DWI fatalities have decreased 44 percent over these past 25 years, saving over 300,000 lives, many hundreds of thousands of injuries and accidents, and hundreds of millions in insurance costs.

Meanwhile, there has been a significant rise in marijuana related accidents and accident fatalities. While many studies demonstrated an impairment in driving motor skills, judgment, and timing, one of the first studies out to predict the degree of driving impairment was a trauma unit outside of Toronto that found that marijuana was the second most common drug found—after alcohol—in the blood of drivers found in highway accidents. They found that 32 percent of drivers brought in had marijuana in their bloodstreams.

A recent study released in 2013 in Colorado, found that from 2006 to 2011, traffic fatalities decreased in Colorado 16 percent, but fatalities involving drivers testing positive for marijuana increased 114 percent.

A newer study was released demonstrating the gravity of the situation. Fatal crashes involving marijuana use tripled during the previous decade, researchers from Columbia University's School of Public Health reported.

A Study utilizing data from the National Highway Traffic Safety Administration's Fatality Analysis Reporting System (FARS) of six states found that while the prevalence of alcohol detected in drivers remained stable throughout a ten year period, cannabinoids were increasingly detected in traffic fatalities and were the most prevalent other drug detected. The study was from six states that routinely perform toxicology tests on drivers in fatal accidents during the period 1999-2010. The greatest increases were for cannabinoids which tripled over the period. Since 2007, cannabinoids have been the most prevalent drug other than alcohol detected in fatally injured drivers. The authors conclude that the "results suggest that drugged driving, specifically driving under the influence of cannabinol…may be playing an increasing role in fatal motor vehicle crashes…" Currently, one of nine drivers involved in fatal crashes would test positive for marijuana," said co-author Dr. Guohua Li, director of the Center for Injury Epidemiology and Prevention at Columbia. The research team drew its conclusions from crash statistics from more than 23,000 drivers who died within one hour of a crash between 1999 and 2010. Drugs played an increasingly prevalent role in fatal crashes, the researchers found, and marijuana proved to be the main drug involved in the increase. The study authors further noted that the combined use of alcohol and marijuana dramatically increases a driver's risk of death. If a driver is under the influence of alcohol, their risk of a fatal crash is 13 times higher than the risk of the driver who is not under the influence of alcohol, "*but if the driver is under the influence of both alcohol and marijuana, their risk increases to 24 times that of a sober person.*"

In the state of Washington, data adapted from the Washington State Patrol and Washington State Toxicologist shows that in 2013, the percentage of total driving cases where the driver tested positive for Carboxy-THC, indicating recent use, rose 33%. Even though Washington State increased its threshold for positive THC from 1 nanogram to over 2 nanograms in 2013, the proportion of positive-THC drivers still increased. This is far greater than percentage increases seen in previous years.

The notion of marijuana as a harmful drug is often downplayed by society but here is one area where the evidence clearly points out that marijuana impairs skills, judgment, reaction time, and decision making faculties—and the end result is an increase in morbidity and mortality for tens of thousands of people.

# MEDICAL MARIJUANA

*"While we see and support a future in the development of chemically defined cannabinoid drugs, we see little future in smoked marijuana as a medicine."*

—John Benson, Co-Principal Investigator for the I.O.M. Report

There are many myths about the "medical" benefits of marijuana. Pro-marijuana enthusiasts are using this to try to legalize raw marijuana, claiming it is good for "medicinal use." In truth, there are numerous problems to this logic.

First, compare marijuana with opium. Pharmaceutical companies have been able to process opium for several medically beneficial drugs such as codeine or morphine, but no doctor would ever advise patients to smoke raw opium. This would present numerous health issues. The same is true for marijuana. There may be several health benefits to processed extracts or constituents from cannabis, but not to the cannabis plant itself in raw form and no doctor—given the dangers of cannabis, should ever recommend the use of raw marijuana. In fact, research is finding out that THC, the psychoactive ingredient in marijuana which causes the "high," itself does not have desired medical properties. Instead, researchers are finding that cannabidiol (CBD) may have the most beneficial properties. Cannabidiol is a major constituent of the cannabis plant, accounting for up to 40% of the plant's extract as a non-psychotropic phytocannabinoid. CBD is considered to have a wider scope of medical applications than THC. It may help as an anti-bacterial agent, in inhibiting cancer cell growth, as a neuro-protective agent, in promoting bone growth, in reducing seizures and convulsions, in reducing blood sugar levels, reducing inflammation, reducing risk of artery blockage, reducing vomiting and nausea, relieving pain and anxiety, in tranquilizing, as a vasorelaxant, etc.

Here we see that under the auspice of the Food and Drug Administration, pharmaceutical research may discover appropriate medications from constituents of cananabis such as CBD, but again, the raw use of marijuana in any form is contra-indicated for health or medical benefit for a wide variety of reasons.

There are over 50 national and state health, criminal justice and human service organizations strongly opposed to legislation that would permit the medicinal use of marijuana in smoked form (MSF.) Essentially, science and experience say that passing "medical" marijuana legislation is bad medicine and bad policy. The Food and Drug Administration along with other agencies in the Health and Human Services Department concluded *that "no sound scientific studies support medical use of marijuana for treatment in the United States, and no animal or human data supported the safety or efficacy of marijuana for general "medical" use."* The American Society of Addiction Medicine, the American Medical Association, American Psychiatric Association, the National Cancer Society, the American College of Physicians (ACP), and over 15 other national organizations are also opposed to MSF. Instead, most recommend that further research should be conducted under the auspice of the Food and Drug Administration into medicines such as current cannabinoid medications including dronabinol (Marinol), Sativex, Epidiolex, and nabilone (Cesamet)—which have shown promise in relieving symptoms of certain illnesses.

Marijuana should be subject to the FDA approval process, which includes clinical trials to determine its efficacy as a medication, a position similar to that of the American Medical Association (AMA), which also stated that marijuana in smoked *form "is unsuitable as a medicine."*

Medical marijuana should not be put forth as a legislative issue. Medicines are not defined by the legislature. In the United States, medications are approved and regulated by the Food and Drug Administration (FDA). The process should be the same for cannabis as for any other drug: clinical trials, recommendations for appropriate use, dosages, purity, and, if approved the drug would be treated as any other medication and dispensed in a pharmacy.

In fact, studies from the Center for Medicinal Cannabis Research in California demonstrated that the side effects exhibited by patients in these studies included adverse central nervous system effects, which resulted in the researchers failing to recommend a "place for cannabis in the treatment armamentarium at this time." The researchers also found that the pain mitigating properties of Marijuana in Smokeable Form (MSF) were not as significant as purported, and other more traditional pharmacological delivery systems would be as, or more, appropriate.

A major study "Early Findings in Controlled Studies of Herbal Cannabis: A Review" (Andrea Barthwell, M.D., FASAM, Journal of Global Drug Policy and Practice, June 24, 2010), concluded that despite the widespread public interest in the therapeutic potential of herbal cannabis…"the data alone fails to make the case that crude, smoked cannabis should be made available to patients."

Many prevention specialists believe—and experience is proving—that the legalization of medical marijuana under many of the proposed conditions could reverse decades of sound prevention and treatment programming and return the country to a state of high drug use. Furthermore, medical marijuana legalization in other states such as California has caused numerous problems and troubles for communities, schools, businesses, homes and families. The actual number of licensed medical marijuana users in California is 553,684—far beyond the "few thousand" projected for true medical need, and the City of Los Angeles saw growth of over 1,000 medical marijuana dispensaries (marijuana cafés.) More youth are using it and it has exacerbated crime. A study examining California's average "medical" marijuana patients found that only 2 percent suffered from AIDS, glaucoma or cancer, and over 97 percent used it for "other" purposes. In California they found that the average "patient" was a 32-year-old white male with a history of drug and alcohol abuse, and no history of a life-threatening disease. Additionally, in Colorado, only 2% of users reported cancer, and less than 1% reported HIV/AIDS as their reason for cannabis.

Proponents of "medical" marijuana even admit that it has become a bad joke, because the use of smoked or eaten crude marijuana in those states that have "medical" marijuana goes well beyond the intent of use for those with designated "serious medical conditions" or elderly people with cancer. One co-author of medical marijuana legislation said, "We created Proposition 215 so that patients would not have to deal with black market profiteers. But today it is all about the money. Most of the dispensaries operating in California are little more than dope dealers with store fronts."

As well, proposed legislation in many states makes it too easy to get marijuana. It is vague and full of loopholes. If you are over age 18, you can obtain marijuana by claiming to have a "serious condition", but the definition of "serious condition" is vague and ambiguous. While it includes "severe debilitating" conditions, it could be defined to include "mental" illness. Yet, if you have such a condition as "dysphoria" you can get marijuana. Dysphoria is anxiety, depression, or restlessness, or simply having an emotional day. Is it really sound health policy to allow people to smoke marijuana simply because they are a little down or restless, or have a simple backache or headache? This is what has happened in other states.

Researchers have found a multitude of problems in states that have legalized medical marijuana. A major study published in Drug and Alcohol Dependence by researchers at Columbia found that residents of states with medical marijuana had marijuana abuse/dependence rates almost twice as high as states without such laws.

A study published in the Harm Reduction Journal analyzed over 3,000 "medical" marijuana users in California, and found that an overwhelming majority (87.9%) of those asked about the details of their marijuana use had initially tried it before the age of nineteen.

Medical marijuana increases DWI. A 2009 National Highway Traffic Safety Administration report found that more people are driving on weekend nights under the influence of marijuana (8.3%) than alcohol (2.2%). Findings demonstrate that even as alcohol traffic fatalities have declined over these years and has now stabilized, marijuana related traffic accident fatalities have risen extraordinarily.

Medical marijuana is being illegally sold. Medical marijuana card holders are dealing the marijuana to non-card holders, to residents in states where the drug is not legal, and to youth (diversion.)

Medical marijuana dispensaries in several states are selling more than just marijuana. Many dispensaries around the country have been caught illegally dealing cocaine, heroin and even weapons such as rifles.

Medical marijuana laws are confusing youth. Young people no longer see marijuana as an illegal drug with harmful effects, but rather as a "natural beneficial herb-based medicine" used to "fix" any ailment.

The THC levels (the active ingredient in marijuana) in medical marijuana are much higher than marijuana sold on the street. This creates a stronger, more intense high especially with the higher THC potency in oils, edibles and new marijuana wax being sold—again without regulation or by prescription.

Under proposed legislation, mental illness including anti-social personality disorder, depression and other life threatening mental disorders are classified as serious conditions and "appropriate" for medical marijuana, even given that the use of marijuana can exacerbate or contribute to mental illness including psychosis and schizophrenia. In fact, the American Psychiatric Association Position Statement on Marijuana as Medicine reads, *"There is no current scientific evidence that marijuana is in any way beneficial for the treatment of any psychiatric disorder. In contrast, current evidence supports, at minimum, a strong association of cannabis use with the onset of psychiatric disorders. Adolescents are particularly vulnerable to harm, given the effects of cannabis on neurological development."* (The position was approved by the APA Assembly on November 2013; and approved by the Board of Trustees December 2013.)

Medical Marijuana is easily diverted to youth. A recent Colorado study shows that 73.8% of youth from adolescent drug treatment programs in the Denver area reported using medical marijuana that had been recommended for someone else (also known as diverted medical marijuana.)

Medial marijuana leads to an increase in addiction, and recovery from marijuana dependency is not easy. One recovering marijuana addict said, *"While I was in California I had a medical marijuana license and couldn't quite smoking. I had to leave the state and go to a state where there was no M.M. program...now I am clean and sober."*

Some proposed legislation is so vague that it can allow marijuana under the guise of medicine to be administered to children since no age limit is identified in the bills. Some bills would also permit pot to be recommended by a variety of practitioners including podiatrists, dentists and veterinarians. Based on the language of one particular bill, animals can potentially be treated with marijuana as well even though animals are highly susceptible to the toxic effects of marijuana. This is just another example of so-called medical marijuana legislation not being well thought out, thus having unintended consequences.

Research also shows that marijuana is a gateway drug and that many marijuana users progress on to greater amounts and stronger drugs. One study demonstrated that the risk for other illicit drug initiation appeared *21 times higher* among cannabis experimenters and 124 times higher among daily cannabis users than among non-users. (Addictive Behaviors February 2012).

Smoked marijuana causes cancer. One of the principle concerns of the use of cannabis, particularly inhaled marijuana, is the carcinogenic potential. It has been implicated in several cancers including lung cancer, prostate and cervical cancer, bladder, testicular germ cell cancer and an increased risk of malignant primary gliomas (2.8 fold or 280% increased risk in people who smoked cannabis once per month or more.) While some have claimed that marijuana has anti-tumor properties, research demonstrates that it is the non-psychoactive cannabinoids—not smoked marijuana—that target the CB2 receptor which may have potential as anti-tumor agents, thus, raw marijuana is not the ideal treatment.

Medical marijuana is used for "chemotherapy." Marijuana legalization advocates would have you believe that smoking marijuana is the only alternative for cancer sufferers who are going untreated for the nausea associated with chemotherapy. However, there are numerous medications and treatments currently available today for these conditions and other illnesses, that may be as, or more, effective and not have the associated negative repercussions.

Another major concern about medical marijuana is that legislation cannot "regulate" or "control" the product. One common cry from marijuana enthusiasts is to legalize, tax and regulate the product. However, such argument presents a spurious picture of the ability of the government to control or regulate medical marijuana especially once it is commercialized. Experience in other states has shown that once legalized, medical marijuana cannot be easily controlled or regulated, resulting in rampant use far beyond the intent of any legislation. For example, "medical" marijuana laws only require a physician's "recommendation" and not a written prescription. Medical marijuana is often sold by storefront dispensaries and not in medically controlled circumstances, and usually patients are not monitored by the physicians after they obtain the recommendation to obtain marijuana. These storefront dispensaries become magnets for crime thus increasing law enforcement costs. There is no quality control. There is no dosage control. There is no diversion control. There is no way to prevent sale to minors. There is no definition of a "serious condition" that absolutely warrants and yet restricts marijuana. There is no way to assure legitimate medical use, versus recreational use to get high.

Medical marijuana regulation is prone to be changed, amended and reduced through further legislation, lawsuits and court decisions. To be sure, as with so many other areas of governmental regulation such as public health, hydrofracking or the alcohol beverage control laws, government "regulation" is a misnomer or rather an objective that can never be fully realized.

Medical marijuana will result in a higher rate of addiction. Plain and simple, marijuana is an addictive drug, and is currently the second most common drug of addiction for admission to treatment programs (alcohol remains the number one drug for treatment admissions.)

With medical marijuana the numbers of users far exceeds estimates. California saw growth far beyond the original projection of users to now over 553,684 licensed marijuana users. The idea that it would be prescribed for only the "few thousand" who were in "acute medical need" was grossly erroneous. Prescriptions have grown and now include everything from anxiety to headaches. Studies have shown that less than 3 percent of licensed users actually have serious diagnoses such as wasting or AIDs. Often, it only takes a telephone call for an "assessment" and a credit card for the assessment fee to secure a medical marijuana license.

Does smoked marijuana really control pain? The finding that marijuana controls pain may be an exaggerated claim. Hospice Net, a nonprofit that provides information and support to patients facing life-threatening illnesses, stated that the pain-relieving effects of marijuana are not consistent, and while marijuana has been reported to reduce anxiety or control nausea so that the person in pain feels better some cancer patients have reported that smoking marijuana actually increased their pain.

Paul Chelminski, MD, MPH, Assistant Professor of Medicine at the University of North Carolina at Chapel Hill, stated that "Several well-designed clinical trials have failed to show any direct benefit of marijuana in relieving pain…"

Fiona Campbell, MD, Assistant Professor in the Department of Anesthesia at the University of Toronto, stated, "We found insufficient evidence to support the introduction of cannabinoids into widespread clinical practice for pain management…"

In fact, the opposite may be true, i.e., marijuana may even increase pain levels. Birgit Kraft, MD, Anesthesiologist in the Department of Special Anesthesia and Pain Therapy at the Medical University of Vienna, concluded in a study, "The surprising result of our study was the absence of any kind of analgesic (pain relieving) activity of THC-standardized cannabis extract…Our results also seem to support the impression that high doses of cannabinoids may even cause increased sensitivity in certain pain conditions."

A major study "Early Findings in Controlled Studies of Herbal Cannabis: A Review" (Andrea Barthwell, M.D., FASAM, Journal of Global Drug Policy and Practice, June 24,

2010), concluded that despite the widespread public interest in the therapeutic potential of herbal cannabis…"the data alone fails to make the case that crude, smoked cannabis should be made available to patients."

Researchers from the Center for Medicinal Cannabis Research in California found that the pain mitigating properties of Marijuana in Smokeable Form (MSF) were not as significant as purported, and other more traditional pharmacological delivery systems would be as, or more, appropriate. Studies also demonstrated that the side effects exhibited by patients included adverse central nervous system effects, which resulted in the researchers failing to recommend a "place for cannabis in the treatment armamentarium at this time."

"Medical" marijuana gives the wrong message to youth. The percentage of U.S. high school seniors reporting past month marijuana use continues to gradually increase, according to recent data from the national Monitoring the Future (MTF) study. In 2012, 22.9% of 12th graders reported using marijuana in the past month, a 25% increase since the most recent low of 18.3% in 2006. While it is far below the peak of 37.1% in 1978, it has returned to a level not seen since the late 1990s. According to the study's principal investigators, one important variable has been a drop in the perception of harm from marijuana use. Analysts suggest that the legalization of medical marijuana—and the idea that marijuana is medicine—has led to the decrease in the perception of harm. It is expected that this notion will lead to future decreases in perception of harm from marijuana use, subsequently resulting in a continuing increase in use by youth.

The "benefits" from medical marijuana may have been grossly overstated. Medical marijuana is no longer appropriate for chronic open-angle glaucoma, for multiple sclerosis, for Alzheimer's disease, or for dementia. Benefits for other conditions are marginal and may be better served with other medications, and given the potential serious side effects/consequences of marijuana use may even be contra-indicated. In fact, in 2013, the American Medical Association (AMA) reiterated their stance against the legalization of marijuana, and the American Psychiatric Association (APA) stated that "There is no current scientific evidence that marijuana is in any way beneficial for the treatment of any psychiatric disorder. In contrast, current evidence supports, at minimum, a strong association of cannabis use with the onset of psychiatric disorders. Adolescents are particularly vulnerable to harm, given the effects of cannabis on neurological development."

Medical marijuana will have an impact on business and industry. States are only now beginning to realize the quagmire inherited with medical marijuana, especially with the array of legal issues under the Americans with Disabilities Act. Employers have already faced lawsuits from employers and potential applicants, who are prescribed medical marijuana. Medical marijuana raises issues for employers such as job performance, lawful hiring practices, and questions pertaining to drug use and drug test results. As marijuana used for medical purposes has the same long term effect on the user as marijuana used for recreation, employees using marijuana can have impairment of short-term memory, attention, motor skills, reaction time, and the organization and integration of complex information. Marijuana use alters perceptions, creates time distortion and can cause drowsiness and lethargy. Heavy marijuana use can cause apathy, decreased motivation, impair cognitive performance and is now clearly associated with causing mental health problems. Employees who use marijuana off-duty are still affected by it on the job. *One study noted that employees who tested positive for marijuana had 55% more industrial accidents and 85% more injuries compared to those that tested negative on a pre-employment exam and they had absenteeism rates 75% higher than those that tested negative.*

Other issues yet to be determined for employers include accommodations that must be made under the Americans with Disabilities Act; accommodations made to a caregiver for a medical marijuana patient; how medical marijuana laws affect drug-free workplace and/or workplace drug testing programs; how medical marijuana affects the rights of employers to protect their interests, property, insurance costs, etc.; as well as the overall question of employer liability.

Medical marijuana has an impact on crime and law enforcement. Since Medical Marijuana was approved in California, the Los Angeles Police Department reported a 200% increase in robberies, 52.2% increase in burglaries, 57.1% rise in aggravated assaults, and a 130.8% rise in burglaries from autos near dispensaries in Los Angeles. Statistics from the Denver Police Department show a 69% percent increase in overall crime at medical marijuana dispensaries, most notably a 75% increase in burglaries compared to one year earlier. The Denver Post reports that 1-in-41 people in Denver are registered medical marijuana patients, and the number of places licensed to sell marijuana products has reached 400 in Denver alone—more than the 375 Starbucks coffee shops statewide. Colorado has also seen a dramatic increase in marijuana related DUIs. Colorado reported that while traffic accidents decreased 16 percent recently, marijuana related DUI traffic fatalities increased 114 percent. Thus, marijuana is now becoming the most dangerous drug in DWIs.

Medical Marijuana will have an effect on the government. Realizing that the Marijuana Clinics could not be regulated and were out of control, the Los Angeles City Council attempted to shut down 423 of the 1,000 Medical Marijuana Clinics and Smokehouses in the city. The ruling was reversed and the closed shops reopened. Government has become impotent to regulate and its creation is out of control. Now communities across the country are trying to invoke "no use" statues in their towns and villages to stop the onslaught of problems caused by medical marijuana clinics. Numerous court decisions and legal challenges are also confounding the problems: In one instance, it was reported that there will be "no penalties for parents who subject their infants and children to secondhand medical marijuana smoke," and in custody situations judges will have no way to "limit visitation rights from marijuana registered parents who are growing or smoking marijuana in their homes." The courts and lawyers will be involved for decades in trying to develop healthy policies as a result of this blunder. Another lawsuit has been filed to sue so that marijuana dispensaries can legally advertise in teen magazines. Thus, the marijuana industry is now expanding to target youth. Additionally, medical marijuana will result in a negative fiscal impact on the state budget through additional services for law enforcement, new regulatory bureaucracies to oversee these programs, more social service costs, higher treatment and rehabilitation costs, higher health care costs, and higher welfare and Medicaid costs. Medical marijuana will eventually cause a quagmire for government and is a program that states can ill afford.

As previously stated, medical marijuana has iatrogenic properties. All drugs have unintended effects and in the world of pharmacology they have iatrogenic effects which are subsequent illnesses or side effects directly resulting from the (attempted) therapeutic use of the drug(s.) These can be more pronounced, and harmful, than any intended "medical" benefit. Thus, when pro-marijuana enthusiasts insist that marijuana has no negative effects to self or others, they are ignoring or minimizing the basic dynamics of pharmacologia, pharmacokinetics, and psychopharmacology (the branch of pharmacology dealing with the psychological effects of drugs.) If a person uses medical marijuana and becomes addicted, as many do, that is an iatrogenic effect and can be a serious violation of medical ethical practice.

Again, marijuana is, simply, not a safe drug. According to the Drug Abuse Warning Network, in 2011 there were over 455,000 marijuana related admissions into hospital emergency rooms. According to the Department of Health and Human Services Treatment Episode Data Set (TEDS), in 2011 there were 333,578 admissions of people into drug treatment programs who stated that marijuana was their primary drug of addiction. In a comprehensive study reported in the international medical journal Lancet, cannabis was found to have negative and harmful consequences to self-or-others, in 15 of the 16 criteria of harmfulness studied. In "Marijuana—Medical Implications" (John R. Hubbard, M.D., Ph.D., Sharonee E. Franco, M.D., and Emmanuel S. Onaivi, Ph.D., Vanderbilt University School of Medicine), the authors listed over 65 effects of marijuana including adverse physical effects and adverse neuropsychiatric effects. Recent Research demonstrates that Marijuana Use Disorder is associated with higher mortality. In fact in one major study, those treated for addiction to cannabis (marijuana) had a higher mortality rate (3.85 times higher than controls), and higher if compared to the death rate risk of cocaine use disorder (2.96), or alcohol use disorder (3.83), although lower than opioid use disorder (5.71) or methamphetamine use disorder (4.67). While some say that marijuana is not as dangerous as alcohol, again this is a spurious statement as marijuana is, itself, a very dangerous drug.

A final study shows that the push to legalize marijuana generally for medicinal purposes is a moot issue. A new study proves that "medical marijuana" bills are not needed. Medical specialists now say that the legalization of raw marijuana as a medicine is no longer a valid legislative item. New research proves that the medical marijuana bills, thought to be dangerous and chaotic for the community, are now found immaterial for medical assistance. The research demonstrated that taking marijuana in a pill form is better for pain relief than smoking it. According to research published in the journal Neuropsychopharmacology, marinol (dronabinol) is an FDA approved cannabinoid medication that provides longer lasting pain relief than smoked marijuana (up to 3-4 hours longer, thus reducing the frequency of times that users need to smoke marijuana.) Secondly, marinol does not provide the "high" as with smoking marijuana. This shows, again, that as with opium, research can produce legitimate beneficial medications without the blanket legalization of an otherwise dangerous drug.

Another concern is the manner of sale proposed in these medical marijuana bills. Marijuana advocates are pushing for marijuana street dispensaries to sell a wide variety of marijuana products. True health policy would allow it to become available through pharmacies, through hospitals, or through the county Department of Public Health, not through street level smoke shops. True health policy would regulate the level of potency and the type of delivery system available.

True health policy would limit any commercialization on this dangerous drug to assure a well regulated and controlled system minimizing any chance of an epidemic of use. True health policy would take every step to minimize abuse and social problems and safeguard public safety. This should be another red flag that the lobby is trying to influence health policy for spurious reasons.

Finally, all medications, particularly those containing controlled substances, should become available only after having satisfied the rigorous criteria of the federal Food and Drug Administration (FDA) approval process. According to David G. Evans, Esq., Executive Director of Drug Free Schools Coalition, "That process has been carefully constructed over the past century to protect patient health and safety. Medical Marijuana legislation violates this rigorous process."

Millions of dollars are spent by pro-marijuana advocates every year to try to legalize medicinal marijuana. There is a sophisticated strategy to negate parents groups and other opposition until such legislation can be passed. Several pro-marijuana groups themselves admitted that the true intent is the full legalization of marijuana for recreational use, and that the legalization of medical marijuana is only the first step toward this goal.

There are legitimate cannabinoid based medications and there may be others in development. But in all circumstances any research and development of medical marijuana as with all drug development, should remain out of the hands of the legislature and be allowed development only under the auspice of the Food and Drug Administration.

# MARIJUANA AND SEXUAL LIBIDO

Marijuana users sometimes report that pot enhances their desire for sex. Some have misnamed it as an aphrodisiac. But a review of research on marijuana and sexual health suggests that male smokers could be courting sexual dysfunction. In one survey male respondents reported that marijuana made them lose interest in sex, feel too lethargic for sex, or be too self-conscious to enjoy it. In another survey respondents blamed marijuana for either losing interest in sex or being unable to have an orgasm at least once during sex while under the influence.

In one study published in the Journal of Psychoactive Drugs, 75 percent of male pot smokers said the drug enhanced their sex lives. However, another study published in the same journal the same year found that erectile dysfunction was twice as common in marijuana users, and other research suggested a dose-response effect—in which small amounts of marijuana may have little impact on sexual dysfunction but more marijuana makes for fewer erections. Sharon Johnson, a professor of social work at the University of Missouri, St. Louis, has studied marijuana use and sexual health. Her study in the Archives of Sexual Behavior (2004), found that marijuana users have both a slightly elevated risk of inhibited orgasms and pain during sex.

In "Marijuana: Medical Implications" (American Family Physician, December 1999), researchers John Hubbard, M.D., PhD., Sharone E. Franco, M.D., and Emmanuel S. Onaivi, PhD., of Vanderbuilt University School of Medicine, stated that an altered libido was a neuropsychiatric adverse effect of marijuana use, and both impotence and reduced testicular size were found to be potential adverse effects of marijuana on the reproductive system.

New research in the Journal of Sexual Medicine by Rany Shamloul, a physician with appointments at the University of Ottawa and Queen's University in Canada, reflects that lab studies show that THC has an inhibitory effect on the smooth muscle of the penis resulting in an effect on the erectile function. According to Shamloul, this suggests that young men may want to think about the long-term effects of marijuana before rolling a joint, "It's a strong message to our younger generations and younger men."

In addition to sexual performance, men who smoke marijuana may find there is a significant decline in reproductive health. Because marijuana leads to decreases in the testosterone levels, the more marijuana one smokes the greater the risk for complications with fertility and reproduction. In fact, sperm count will be notably smaller in the man who smokes marijuana regularly and may even lead to sterility.

Finally, one essential component of an intense sexual experience is the intimacy it provides. Yet several reports suggest that the effects of marijuana heighten one's "personal space," and therefore, can emotionally distance partners instead of bringing them closer together in a romantic bond. Similar to having sex while being intoxicated with alcohol, sex while intoxicated with marijuana is the same—just sex instead of romance.

In general marijuana's sexual effects are not fully known, but do include sex-inhibiting characteristics even to the point of marijuana induced impotence.

# THE ECONOMIC IMPACTS OF MARIJUANA LEGALIZATION

In an article published in the January 2014 issue of The Journal of Global Drug Policy and Practice, David Evans, Esq., Executive Director of the Drug Free Projects Coalition presented a compelling case for maintaining a continued stance of illegality toward the possession, manufacturing and use of recreational marijuana.

For this study, Evans analyzed all data to explore the economic and social costs associated with marijuana legalization. His study acknowledged the growth in income and revenue generated by marijuana legalization. However, where other studies stop there, he proceeded to also measure the environmental, medical, criminal, spiritual, productivity and other social costs—in short the human costs—of legalization.

Evans reviewed the pro-legalization arguments of cost savings from reduced imprisonment, projected revenues from taxes and streams of income, and immediate and projected expenditures to address the known harms of marijuana use and to implement and enforce policy reforms. He confirmed several of the propositions with empirical data, and also spoke to other unanticipated findings—such as that economists predict use of marijuana will subsequently increase by up to 289 percent with legalization (and perhaps greater.)

Evans reports that many of these benefits will be offset by additional costs, for instance as related to DUI/DWI as legalization will entail additional spending to update and enforce drugged driving regulations because there is evidence that consuming marijuana before driving doubles the chances of collision.

Evans concludes that recent estimates of legalization's impact on government spending predict possible savings and revenues but these estimates are incorrect as they do not reflect the economic costs of departing from current policy. The true fiscal impact will depend on the costs generated by repealing current laws, plus the costs of implementing and enforcing proposed reforms, minus any tax revenues and savings that might accrue. Repealing current laws will generate additional costs due to consequences stemming from the increase in marijuana use, abuse, and dependence. The study reviews the known harms of marijuana use including public health, safety, and mental and physical effects, and healthcare costs in general.

Evans concludes that legalization will not only have devastating consequences for health, crime, and productivity, it is a waste of taxpayer dollars that could much more wisely be spent on more effective deficit-reducing measures.

His conclusion by the data is that "Not all the data is in about the economics of marijuana legalization, but on balance it would be a negative public policy for which our society will pay a great spiritual, medical, public safety and economic cost that we can ill afford."

# THE DIFFERENCES BETWEEN ALCOHOL AND MARIJUANA

What seems to be continually confused and misconstrued in the marijuana "debate" is alcohol's comparison to marijuana. The logic perpetuated by the pro-marijuana advocates is that "alcohol is more dangerous than marijuana, therefore, as alcohol is legal so should be marijuana" (as it is a less dangerous drug.)

This premise cannot stand under rational dialogue. At the very least as a logic statement this argument is not logically valid because the logic form leads to a false premise, and thus, to a false conclusion.

The fact is that there are enormous differences between alcohol and marijuana, and even if there were not, one still could not say that "because arsenic is less toxic that cyanide it should be legalized."

Alcohol is classified as a depressant drug, and marijuana—well, actually has no classification. Marijuana has depressant properties, but also stimulant properties. It is neither a narcotic, nor a pure hallucinogen. It is neither an anti-depressant, steroid, hormone, antiseptic, barbiturate or benzodiazepine, antibiotic, enzyme, statin, nor a vasodilator. Marijuana, simply, is a species of the *Cannabaceae* family of plants. The best classification of marijuana is that as a "pseudo euphorohallucinogen." So one really cannot compare alcohol and marijuana, as is it like comparing apples to oranges.

The greatest difference, though, is that the vast majority of drinkers—some 80 percent, use alcohol rarely or lightly and not to the point of intoxication. In fact, intoxication by alcohol is discouraged by every reputable health profession in the country. The vast majority of people are either non-drinkers or "social drinkers"—light to moderate and will have a beer at a football game, or a glass of wine with dinner. In this regard alcohol is not like marijuana because the objective of the drinker is not to detach oneself from reality by overindulging to intoxication, something that society shuns and health professionals reject.

But marijuana users do not use marijuana for the flavor. They do not use it to quench thirst. They do not use it to foster extroversion. That is because the primary purpose of smoking marijuana is to get high. It is strictly about the psychoactive effects. When marijuana is sold, the dealer won't tell you about his bud's "culinary scents with a hint of peppermint." He's going to tell you how fast and how long you will get high. The marijuana user has one objective—to get intoxicated, and the new brands and strains continuously build the THC content to achieve more and more of this goal.

This is where the problem lies: if people are either drinking or smoking to get high, then there is a problem. Marijuana users are really using for intoxication—for impairment… which is analogous to *dysfunction.*

*So, the key difference between alcohol and marijuana is that one can have a glass of wine without becoming "intoxicated" or mentally impaired. The whole point of smoking marijuana, however, is to become "intoxicated" (high) and impair the mental state of the mind. And that is physically, mentally, emotionally and spiritually dysfunctional and unacceptable.*

Second, one really doesn't drink alcohol, they drink flavored water with alcohol in it. With alcohol, the alcohol concentration is not the most critical factor in alcoholic beverage consumption. Alcohol comes in, literally, thousands of distinct flavors, all with varying ranges of alcohol present. Most often people choose to drink simply for the taste and not the effect. People go on wine-tasting tours not to get high, but find a wine that they enjoy the flavor of. The same is simply not true of marijuana.

Third, with long term use light drinking hasn't had damaging effects while marijuana use is more likely to cause, exacerbate, or contribute to problems like thinking impediments, memory loss, cognitive deficiencies, depression, anxiety, dependency, and (if smoked) smoking-related health problems such as throat and lung cancer and respiratory problems. Social drinking, i.e., low-level alcohol consumption (0.01-0.03 percent BAC) is consistent with most manual and intellectual tasks; and alcohol has several physical properties such as being easily metabolized and eliminated by the body. The same is not true for marijuana. The effects of regular marijuana consumption are quite different from alcohol. For example, the National Institute on Drug Abuse has released studies showing that use of marijuana has wide-ranging negative health effects. Long-term marijuana consumption "impairs the ability of T-cells in the lungs' immune system to fight off some infections." These studies have also found that marijuana consumption impairs short-term memory, making it difficult to learn and retain information or perform complex tasks; slows reaction time and impairs motor coordination; increases heart rate by 20 percent to 100 percent, thus elevating the risk of heart attack; and alters moods, resulting in artificial euphoria, calmness, or (in high doses) anxiety or paranoia. Marijuana has toxic properties that can result in birth defects, pain, respiratory system damage, brain damage, and stroke. Further, prolonged use of marijuana may cause cognitive degradation and is "associated with lower test scores and lower educational attainment because during periods of intoxication the drug affects the ability to learn and process information, thus influencing attention, concentration, and short-term memory."

Also, unlike alcohol, marijuana has been shown to have a residual effect on cognitive ability that persists beyond the period of intoxication. According to the National Institute on Drug Abuse, whereas alcohol is broken down relatively quickly in the human body, THC is stored in organs and fatty tissues allowing it to remain in a user's body for days or even weeks after consumption. Research has shown that marijuana consumption may also cause "psychotic symptoms." According to the British Lung Foundation, "smoking three or four marijuana joints is as bad for your lungs as smoking twenty tobacco cigarettes." Researchers in Canada found that marijuana smoke contains significantly higher levels of numerous toxic compounds, like ammonia and hydrogen cyanide, than regular tobacco smoke. In fact, the study determined that ammonia was found in marijuana smoke at levels of up to 20 times the levels found in tobacco. Similarly, hydrogen cyanide was found in marijuana smoke at concentrations three to five times greater than those found in tobacco smoke. And yes, marijuana is addictive. One study found that more than 30 percent of adults who used marijuana in the course of a year were dependent on the drug. These individuals often show signs of withdrawal and compulsive behavior. Today, marijuana is linked to a variety of crimes including assault and murder, and drug-related crime. According to a study by the RAND Corporation, approximately 60 percent of arrestees test positive for marijuana use in the United States, England, and Australia. Further, marijuana metabolites are found in arrestees' urine more frequently than those of any other drug. So it seems as though there are significant differences even with long term low-level alcohol use and marijuana use.

To equate marijuana use with alcohol consumption is, at best, uninformed and, at worst, actively misleading. Furthermore, to state that "since alcohol is legal so should marijuana be as it is less dangerous" presents a faulty logic model—something that chemically impaired thinking produces.

# THE LEGALIZATION OF MARIJUANA IN COLORADO: THE IMPACT

The Rocky Mountain High Intensity Drug Trafficking Area (RMHIDTA) published a preliminary report on the impact of marijuana legalization in the state of Colorado, utilizing a comparison of three different eras in Colorado's legalization history: 2006-2008 (early medical marijuana era), 2009-2012 (medical marijuana expansion era), and 2012-present (medical marijuana expansion and recreational use era.)

The purpose of this report was to document the impact of the legalization of marijuana for medical and recreational use in Colorado. The report tried to collect comparative data in a variety of areas, including but not limited to: traffic fatalities; youth marijuana use; adult marijuana use; emergency room admissions; marijuana-related exposure cases; and diversion of Colorado marijuana outside the state. (Source: The Legalization of Marijuana in Colorado: The Impact (Volume 1), Rocky Mountain High Intensity Drug Trafficking Area (RMHIDTA), August 2013.)

The preliminary findings were both revealing and disturbing:

Colorado Driving Fatalities: From 2006 to 2011, traffic fatalities decreased in Colorado 16 percent, but fatalities involving drivers testing positive for marijuana increased 114 percent.

Colorado Youth Marijuana Use: In 2011, the national average for youth 12-to-17 years old considered "current" marijuana users was 7.64 percent which was the highest average since 1981. The Colorado average percent was 10.72.

Colorado Adult Marijuana Use: In 2011, the national average for young adults ages 18-to-25 considered current marijuana users was at 18.7 percent. The Colorado average was 27.26 percent.

Colorado Emergency Room—Marijuana Admissions: From 2005 through 2008 there was an average of 741 visits per year to the emergency room in Colorado for marijuana-related incidents involving youth. That number increased to 800 visits per year between 2009 and 2011.

Colorado Marijuana-Related Exposure Cases: From 2005 through 2008, the yearly average number of marijuana-related exposures for children ages 0-to-5 years was 4. For 2009 through 2012, that number increased 200 percent.

Diversion of Colorado Marijuana (General): From 2005 to 2008, compared to 2009 to 2012, interdiction seizures involving Colorado (as a source state for marijuana being sent to other parts of the country), marijuana quadrupled from an average per year of 52 to 242. During the same period, the average number of pounds of Colorado marijuana seized per year increased 77 percent from an average of 2,220 to 3,937 pounds. A total of 7,008 pounds was seized in 2012.

Diversion of Colorado Marijuana (Postal Packages): In 2010, the U.S. Postal Inspection Service seized 15 packages with Colorado marijuana destined for other states. Seizures steadily increased through 2012 when 158 parcels were seized.

From 2010 to 2012 Colorado marijuana seized by the U.S. Postal Inspection Service increased from 57 to 262 pounds.

Suicide: Also, Colorado has now set an unfortunate record with the highest number of suicides ever recorded in state history—now at a 30 year high—with the Rocky Mountain Region having the highest rates in the country!

So far, the legalization experiment in Colorado has proven to be a very bad decision for the health, safety and welfare of the people of that state.

# THE WAR ON DRUGS

Another myth about marijuana is that the "war on drugs has failed" and should be abandoned for a more humane "treatment" approach for marijuana addicts. Again, the logic premise supporting this opinion is faulty, but unfortunately too many people are uninformed and buying into this 30 second sound bite.

As a comparison, look at the "war on poverty" started by President Johnson in 1964. The official federal poverty rate at that time approximated nineteen percent. Today there is still an unacceptable level of poverty in the United States, one of the wealthiest countries in the world. The poverty rate stands at thirteen percent.

Did the war on poverty fail? No. The strategies employed both effectively and significantly decreased the poverty rate for millions. It also raised the standard of living and quality of life for millions more although they may still remain in poverty, i.e., they have food, and in most cases shelter, and basic health coverage if needed. They moved from absolute poverty to relative poverty. The "war" was a descriptive term that encompassed a number of economic and social strategies and although it needs to be continued and strengthened, overall, it had significant success.

Another example is the "war on illiteracy." The problem with illiteracy and the associated social issues are tremendous, and that is why numerous presidents began to support reading programs, Head Start programs, remedial training programs, strengthening libraries, and curricula development initiatives beginning in 1985 and even before. According to one study by the Department of Education, in 2003 the level of functional illiteracy in the U.S. was about 14 percent.

Does this mean that the "war" failed? Not at all. In fact, the level of "pure" illiteracy dropped significantly from the levels of the nineteenth century. Furthermore, there are increasing rates of school attendance, rising proportions of adults completing high school, and rising proportions attending college. Progressively fewer adults have limited their education to completion of the 8th grade which was typical in the early part of the twentieth century, and today, 86 percent of people are high school graduates, and 29 percent hold a 4 year college degree. The "war" on illiteracy has not been won, but certainly great gains have been made.

Similarly, the "war on drugs" has seen great strides. The term "war," again, is a misnomer, and people do not understand the full model. The term "war on drugs" applies to a campaign with several strategies: the prohibition of illegal drug manufacturing, use, and distribution of those drugs; military aid and military intervention for supply side decreases—also called interdiction; local and state law enforcement and criminal justice strategies; legislation and policy initiatives; and funding for drug prevention and for drug treatment programs for demand side decreases. The "war" actually is comprised of all components. The war on drugs is not singular, but is a multi-pronged, multi-phasic strategy and not just a military operation.

The term "war on drugs" was popularized by the media shortly after a press conference given on June 18, 1971, by

President Richard Nixon during which he declared drug abuse "public enemy number one." That message to the Congress included text about devoting more federal resources to the "prevention of new addicts, and the rehabilitation of those who are addicted", but that part did not received the same public attention as the term "war on drugs."

Of course the federal government supports drug abuse prevention and treatment programs and recognizes them as a vital part of the armamentarium of strategies for reducing drug use, but to be most successful this "war" does need a multi-faceted approach including international collaboration and yes, military operations.

Drug enthusiasts would have one believe, however, that all that is needed are treatment programs for those who do succumb to addiction. Most certainly treatment programs are a necessary component of a successful health policy, but as a stand alone program treatment would be sure to fail as accessibility and availability of drugs increased.

As well, the question remains, did the "war" on drugs fail? The answer is a resounding "No!" Similar to poverty and illiteracy, this strategy be it called a war or a campaign or any other name, needs to be constant and dynamic for success. The use of illegal drugs was at an all time high in 1978. Since then, the combination of efforts at all levels—federal, state and local brought drug abuse down to a new low for modern society in 2006. This is especially encouraging since by its nature drug use is progressive and should have increased significantly over that 35 year period. So instead of increasing as analysts would have predicted, the overall drug policy strategy actually decreased drug abuse by over 50 percent.

Did the "war" totally eliminate drug abuse? No, but no strategy ever will. The goal for the war on poverty, the war on illiteracy and the war on drugs is to make *significant and realistic progress in reducing these social ills*—in no way can anyone defend with any degree of credibility that these three issues will ever be fully resolved.

Finally, the question remains is it worth the investment of billions of dollars? Again, the answer is yes. In the "war on disease", the investment of billions of dollars helped to fight the three other most critical health problems for Americans: the cancer epidemic, heart disease, and diabetes. Although these, also, have not been eliminated great strides have been made and countless lives saved.

The "war" on disease also helps to minimize a host of other illnesses and diseases like muscular dystrophy and mental illness—and once in awhile this war helps to fully eradicate an illness such as polio. Similarly, the war on drugs also helps to minimize other social problems caused by drug use, minimizes drug related health and mental health problems, drug related family dysfunction, drug related job loss, license loss, bankruptcy, it lowers business costs, and lowers any of a number of secondary drug related social problems. Anyone would fully agree that the war against disease and illness is one to continue to fund utilizing the public health model (addressing both the host, agent and environment.)

With that, the war against illiteracy, the war against poverty, and the war against drugs, similarly, need to be maintained. These are the wars our families need.

# MARIJUANA AS A BIOHAZARD

When one thinks of biohazards, the most immediate thought is a biological military weapon used in war. Generally, however, biohazards include a wide variety of objects that present a risk or potential risk to the health of humans, animals, or the environment. The risk can be direct, potential, or through the environment.

Most biohazards are classified as pathogens, infectious diseases, viruses, bacteria, "superbugs", parasites, prions, allergens, venoms, and hundreds of other microorganisms. Biohazards can include, though, any infectious agents or hazardous biological materials including biological waste, medical wastes or contaminants, discarded vaccines and medications, human or animal tissues or fluids, certain chemicals, venomous wildlife or insects, certain diseases, or select agents. *Biohazards also include poisonous plants.*

The key element is that biohazards are biologically active agents that may cause illness or disease in other living organisms or cause significant impact to the environment or community.

Given this definition, is it possible that marijuana should be labeled by the Environmental Protection Agency (EPA) as a biohazard? If one accepts the premise that marijuana has toxic and noxious properties, then perhaps the inclusion of marijuana is not implausible.

If one can define marijuana as a biohazard then one can begin to determine the biorisk. The "Biorisk" is the combination of the likelihood of the occurrence of an adverse event involving exposure to a biological agent or toxin, and the consequence of such an exposure. With more research, scientists may actually be able to develop a formula for the adverse side effects of marijuana use as well as the consequences of such exposure.

There are two areas in which marijuana may be considered for classification as a biohazard.

First, marijuana may be radioactive. Researchers have long known that cigarette smoking produces pronounced radioactive exposure, most specific to radioactive Polonium 210 depending upon soil conditions and fertilizer use. But marijuana contains Potassium 40, a radioactive isotope of potassium. Although the level of the isotope is low and the radiation exposure is very small it may still be a factor especially as it is inhaled into the lungs. In fact, the Border Patrol looks for and often catches trucks full of marijuana using sophisticated gamma radiation detection equipment at the airports and border crossings, which detects the radioactive element in the hidden marijuana shipments.

A second concern is that experts say that there is a considerable amount of "contaminated chemicals" in marijuana. According to one testing organization for dispensaries in California, there are many chemicals and pesticides used in marijuana growing which threaten the health of marijuana users. There are no application standards enforced. Growers will often use anything including chemicals or pesticides intended only for lawns or other non-edibles to apply to pot plants. *Medical cannabis samples collected in Los Angeles have been found to contain pesticide residues at levels 1600 times the legal digestible amount.* Again, because marijuana is consumed (inhaled or eaten), any toxins it carries have an even more direct route into the lungs and/or blood stream, and the situation may be more disturbing for individuals with health problems who smoke marijuana where the risk of pesticide exposure could worsen the individual's health problems or could make them more vulnerable.

As an aside, marijuana is not environmentally friendly. Marijuana growing is not a green industry. Studies have shown that growing marijuana indoors leaves a significant carbon footprint. Marijuana is a "power-hungry" crop, intense in the use of electricity according to a study in the journal Energy Policy. Producing one joint indoors is equivalent to leaving a light bulb on for 25 hours, and producing 2.2 pounds of marijuana indoors, one study says, is equivalent to driving across country seven times.

Again, marijuana is toxic to pets and animals. Marijuana smoke is dangerous to the lungs. Second hand smoke or sidestream smoke is dangerous. Marijuana use is dangerous if used by a pregnant women and passed on to her developing fetus. Marijuana is dangerous as passes through breast milk to a baby. Marijuana is not environmentally friendly. It has side effects. It is addictive and dangerous to humans. By any and all of these accounts, perhaps one day marijuana will be recognized as a biohazard. It certainly fits the definition.

# MARIJUANA AND IDOLATRY

There are numerous studies showing that the practice of religion by youth and families is a protective factor against drug abuse. In fact, one review of over 150 studies on drug and alcohol abuse found that people who are more highly religious are less likely to use substances and less likely to experience substance-related consequences. These studies have a predictive value for prevention.

There are numerous studies showing the positive role of religion and spirituality in treatment and long term recovery for drug addiction. These studies have a predictive value for long term recovery and evidence-based treatment plans.

The greater question, however, is to what extent do marijuana users replace God with the drug? Generally speaking, it is found that drug and alcohol use is highest in non-religious groups. It is also speculated that drug users traditionally are, or become, non-practitioners in traditional religions or religious practices. In one study of 1,178 current users of illicit drugs and 389 former users, it was found that attending religious services and the importance of religion were negatively associated with the use of alcohol, marijuana, cocaine, and hallucinogens.

People who do not have consistent religious practices are more likely to use drugs, but also people who use drugs are less likely to engage in or maintain consistent religious practices.

In fact, many use drugs to a point of obsession almost worshiping them in lieu of belief and practice of worship in God. The word "idol" usually conjures up images of figurines on an altar or statues of gods in a temple with people bowing down to them, and sacrificing their money or their goods. Many see this behavior as entirely inconceivable in today's modern society for any other purpose than a religious practice, and yet, millions of drug users place their trust and dependence—their faith and their hopes, their money and their goods in a drug. As well, often there is a ritual of use with drugs which mimics religious worship customs.

Without realizing it, the objects of an addiction become the objects of worship. That is called idolatry. Drugs, for millions, have become functional gods. In fact, many marijuana users will testify that they use marijuana in part to seek a higher consciousness, a connection with a higher power. Yet, this connection becomes self-centered, is counterfeit, and lacks in total fulfillment and the expression of joy especially when the effects of marijuana drug wears off.

One of the commandments states, "Thou shalt not have false idols, i.e., you shall not make for yourself an idol in the form of anything in heaven above or on the earth beneath or in the waters below. You shall not bow down to them or worship them." People turn to idols because they are seeking something—some pleasure or comfort or connection apart from God. When trials and troubles come, when people experience emotional or physical pain, when they are lonely or bored, where do they turn for comfort and solace, for understanding, for satisfaction and joy? Marijuana users, more so, do not turn to God but to the drug.

Alcoholism and drug addiction are impacting families and communities around the world. Here in affluent America, we are drinking and drugging ourselves to death. According to Joseph Califano, former President of the National Center on Addiction and Substance Abuse at Columbia University, America has 4 percent of the world's population but consumes two-thirds of the world's illegal drugs.

Over the past decade, considerable research has emerged that demonstrates the benefits of religious practice within society. Religious practice promotes the well-being of individuals, families, and the community. Regular attendance at religious services is linked to healthy, stable family life, strong marriages, and well-behaved children. The practice of religion also leads to a reduction in the incidence of domestic abuse, crime, substance abuse, and addiction. Religious practice also leads to an increase in physical and mental health, longevity, and education attainment.

The problem, however, is that marijuana use interrupts the awareness of, understanding of, and conscious practice of religion, faith and worship of God. In its place we find an over-valuing of a drug, and too often an over-reliance on that drug to the exclusion of everything else—family, friends, work and even God.

At the very least marijuana use to the point of intoxication could be called gluttony (one of the seven deadly sins.) But when it is marijuana that the user venerates and depends upon to the level of the exclusion of God, perhaps it can even be called idolatry.

# MARIJUANA IS PET ABUSE

Studies in the early 1970s warned of hazards to animals, most specifically monkeys and rats, with the administration of large amounts of marijuana (THC.) These studies found a variety of effects including moderately severe central nervous system depression, mild hyperactivity, dose related chronic convulsions, and cumulative toxicity and even death. Again, these doses were much higher than those for human consumption, but behavioral, clinical, hematological and hemochemical changes were noted, as well as induced inflammation in the cerebellum, which resulted in learning and coordination problems. This toxicity to animals is probably one of the reasons that animals tend to refuse to self-administer THC, and this may be worth further note to say that marijuana use is not a natural instinct but rather a learned behavior.

Today, veterinarians across the country are starting to warn marijuana users to be sure to prevent exposure of marijuana to their pets. Vets are finding that increasingly pets are being brought to them in toxic conditions and while a person may not die from marijuana use, pets can and do.

What further complicates this is that some people believe it is funny to get their dog stoned. Not only is this not funny, but it is now considered to be pet abuse.

THC is toxic to pets, and exposure to marijuana can result in a very sick animal.

Vets are reporting that the vast majority of pet exposure occurs in dogs (95 percent). While studies show that animals do not self-select to eat marijuana, dogs are known for eating a wide variety of foods and food-like substances. In this case, the most common way of ingestion is eating MIPs (Marijuana Infused Products), i.e., marijuana cookies, brownies, butter, or other marijuana edibles. These are very tempting to animals. Additionally, pets can also be exposed to second-hand marijuana smoke.

Similar to human intoxication, THC is rapidly absorbed into the bloodstream of animals and signs of marijuana toxicity typically become apparent within minutes to a few hours. The most common signs of toxicity for animals are neurologic abnormalities, including stumbling that may progress to an inability to walk, depression, agitation, dribbling urine, twitching, seizures, pupil dilation and occasionally coma. About 30 percent of animals exposed to THC will develop gastrointestinal signs including drooling, vomiting and diarrhea. Some animals become highly agitated from marijuana, while others exhibit signs of depression. Some may experience seizures. Others showed signs of lethargy, diarrhea, and acting strange like making strange vocalizations. Approximately one-third of animals exposed to marijuana will develop signs of nausea and vomiting. Death is rare but can occur. These effects may last for days as THC is slowly released from fat and metabolized.

Different from human consumption, however, marijuana exposure in pets causes a neurologic toxicity which is not like the "high" that people experience, and the symptoms (staggering, agitation, stupor, etc.) that develop in pets do not appear enjoyable for them.

Depending on the circumstances the veterinarian may try to give a medication to induce vomiting or administer activated charcoal to help limit further absorption of THC. The pet may need hospitalization and care including an intravenous catheter, IV fluids, and monitoring of vital signs. Again, depending, more aggressive care may also be needed.

Finally, animals that had been chronically administered THC can suffer a range of withdrawal symptoms, including paw tremors, "wet-dog shakes" and other disorganized behavior.

Dr. Stacy Meola, a veterinarian in Wheat Ridge, helped with a study that shows that the number of dogs that fell ill to marijuana has quadrupled in Colorado since medical marijuana became legalized. Vets caution to keep marijuana away from pets, and in instances of suspected THC ingestion take them in and be honest with the vet.

If you are concerned that your pet ingested marijuana, contact your veterinarian or call the 24-hour Animal Poison Control Center available throughout the U.S. and Canada for pet owners and veterinary professionals who require assistance with treating a potentially poisoned pet at 800-213-6680.

It is not funny to give a dog marijuana. Ingesting marijuana can be life-threatening to a dog or at the very least a "bad trip," a terrifying and dangerous experience for an animal.

# THE MYTH OF "TAX, REGULATE, AND CONTROL"

There is a particularly troublesome sound bite seemingly gaining support around the country. It is to legalize marijuana and "tax, regulate and control" it. Perhaps in a well principled and orderly world where capitalism and commercialism is not the golden ring prize, this might be a possibility to consider.

In reality, there are several absolutes which would neutralize any realistic attempt to tax, regulate and control marijuana. First, the tax revenue raised on marijuana would never meet the increased social costs that would result from the increase in users. The nation's experiences with alcohol and tobacco show that for every dollar gained in taxes, the nation spends $10 on health care and social costs. The same would be true for marijuana related social costs.

With increased use of marijuana, government costs would increase. Welfare costs, criminal justice costs, and health care costs would increase. Insurance costs, and direct and indirect costs to business and industry would all increase. There would be more addiction centers. There would be greater use of emergency rooms and hospitals. Mental health clinics would need to hire many more staff. Property taxes would increase. School taxes would increase as schools would need to hire more specialists and special needs teachers. The actual costs would rise dramatically, above and beyond the tax dollars raised through legalization. The economic argument for legalization based upon increased tax revenue collapses when all accounting is considered. Then there is the human cost—the pain and suffering of addiction, the loss of lives, of the quality of life, and in potential years of life lost on top of this. These costs are harder to quantify, but are much more substantial than the simple economics.

Second, there is no regulation or control feature that is an absolute. There is no way to regulate and control marijuana once it is legalized. This is, yet, another fallacy in a long list of misbeliefs about marijuana. Even now communities are trying to fight back to stop the marijuana growth in their communities but without success. Lawsuits are placed to ever expand marijuana dispensaries and users rights and challenge the laws that do control and regulate. Pro-marijuana advocates are always there to challenge and change the control criteria, and legislators change bills to expand the law. It truly is the opening of Pandora's Box.

There are numerous examples where seemingly competent governmental and business organizations failed to meet their regulatory and control obligations—and people suffered disastrous consequences. The government failed to effectively regulate the mortgage and banking industry's use of subprime mortgage loans and unregulated financial instruments called "credit default swaps", which set off a series of events and conditions that led to the financial crisis and recession of 2008. The FDA failed to realistically regulate the new classes of prescription pain medication narcotics, and the country experienced an epidemic of prescription drug abuse and addiction. The SEC failed to regulate Bernie Madoff's investment schemes until it was too late. The Federal Aviation

Administration regulates air traffic, yet there have been over 150 planes landing at the wrong airport over these past years.

With the alcohol industry there are also "tight" regulations, yet, every year there are many thousands of violations of the Alcohol Beverage Control (ABC) laws. Minors are still served alcohol (in as much as 50 percent of the stores/bars.) Intoxicated individuals are still served alcohol even though it is against the law to serve intoxicated individuals. The industry continues to challenge state liquor authorities to reduce taxes, reduce regulations, reduce licensing restrictions, expand alcohol percentages, and to increase the number of alcohol beverage sites, sales venues, and alcohol percentage standards. One government bureaucrat stated that they are so understaffed that their department cannot even accommodate the most necessary audit functions, much less monitor and enforce the multitude of other regulations and violations. So with the alcohol industry there really is no serious taxation, there really is no true accountability in the regulation, and the control is often left up to the business itself (i.e., self-control and self-monitoring by a sector with conflicting interests)—certainly not a formal and genuine manner of professional operation.

Of course one of the most highly regulated areas of government is the traffic system. Yet each year law enforcement officers issue 41 million speeding tickets because people do not follow the law—and assumingly, there are tens of millions of others who speed but do not get caught. Here, regulation—even with "taxation" (fines and surcharges) and controls, simply does not work as well as one would otherwise expect.

Did government regulations prevent the tobacco industry from adding extra nicotine into tobacco to enhance the addition potential? Did government regulations prevent the 250 deaths and more than 3,000 serious injuries due to faulty tires in the Ford/Firestone scandal? Did government regulations prevent the use of poisonous chemicals in hydrofracking? Have government regulations fully prevented faulty manufacturing and recalls of cars, or contaminated blood supplies, or food poisoning, or computer hacking?

Regulators always fail at times in auditing, monitoring and enforcing directives and regulations. This is because there will never be enough government officials to monitor and enforce the regulations needed, and because businesses and industries try to "get around" the regulations for profit enhancing reasons. One representative from a health insurance company said (in response to the Affordable Care Act) *"There is no law that Congress can make that we can't find a way around."*

This too, will happen with the marijuana industry. Youth will be served, adults will be served too much, and any regulation and control features will become a secondary consideration. As well, the industry will start to commercialize and then to market and promote—even to youth. In fact it has been reported that even now marijuana food and candy are being marketed to children and are already responsible for a growing number of marijuana-related emergency room visits by children. Marijuana edibles with names such as "Ring Pots" and "Pot Tarts" are inspired by common candy and dessert products appealing to children. Also, several profitable vending machines containing products such as marijuana brownies are emerging.

With legalization and commercialization marijuana will fast become the "Big Tobacco" of our time—"Big Marijuana." This is one of the areas where "tax, regulate and control" is a fantasy, and an ideal which can never be realized in totality.

# THE THROES OF MARIJUANA ADDICTION

One woman, in her reflections, said that marijuana robbed her of a decent life. She found it to be a very antisocial and paranoid drug that made her confused and think and act stupidly. It led her into alcohol, then harder drugs and then a life of crime to support her addictions. She became addicted to marijuana and regrets the day she ever picked it up. In her words she became a slave to it, and it cost her 25 years of wasted life—15 years of which was spent in prison. Her message to all teenagers is to be smarter than she was—"don't destroy your life with addiction by picking up that first joint."

Educators, coaches, law enforcement personnel, health professionals and researchers can all teach about the dangers of drugs. The stories shared by marijuana users, themselves, however, present perhaps the greatest and most compelling educational life lessons one can learn. There are millions of these stories to be told, and yet, most of our young adults hear few if any—or do not have parents who help them process the information on a deeper, reality-based level.

The earliest experiences of several users can only begin to highlight the real dangers. One woman, Jane, smoked pot after having come out of an abusive relationship. Each time she did she suffered incredible panic attacks and relived the situation (pseudo-flashbacks), and needed to call for help to "talk her down." Jane became hysterical, simply, whenever she used pot. Similarly, Jim had lost a close family member and smoking pot would send him into a deep-introverted and isolating depression. Nathan was very high one night and date raped a girl. Dick was a college student that developed an atypical psychosis after beginning to smoke marijuana. Paul started to develop delusions of persecution when he smoked.

Then there are the "more serious" examples. Pete started using marijuana as a teenager and later became a full alcoholic with five DWIs, a lifetime pattern of failed marriages, and a carefree (and careless), no responsibility attitude.

Charlie, a veteran, became suicidal and would be admitted into a psychiatric center for several months every time he began to smoke. When he was clean he was a very social, upbeat person with a solid family and friends but when he began to smoke it changed his personality and caused a deep dark place to which he submerged and was unable to help himself out—often for months at a time.

Tom was an excellent college student, and again, a friendly, helpful person who had everyone's affection. Tom smoked marijuana everyday through college, but graduated on time and with average marks. Tom continued to smoke and a few years later Tom had a catastrophic nervous breakdown that all but destroyed him, his career, and his family life as well. He never fully recovered from that breakdown.

Sam, similarly, was warm, friendly and funny, but his marijuana use caused a pronounced amotivational syndrome whereby he could not hold a job nor had any way to support himself, had never married, and had no interests or hobbies at all. Years later he had absolutely nothing to show for his life. A true life wasted on marijuana and the pursuit of an ideal he never found. This was one of the greatest tragedies—the wasting of human potential.

Another real tragedy was Jennie. Jennie was the director of a social service health center and was, herself, an excellent psychiatric social worker that had helped—literally—hundreds of people. Jennie, a loving mother of three and a devoted wife began to smoke marijuana at a social gathering. In a relatively short period of time she developed a severe depression, which she tried to medicate with—yes—marijuana. The depression became profound. She began to try every treatment known in psychiatric circles, but the darkness would not lift. She began to try holistic practices, but the darkness would not lift. She began to try new age techniques and spiritualism—but the darkness would not lift. She changed to an organic diet. She changed her work schedule for stress reduction. She manipulated every aspect of her life except one—she continued to smoke marijuana. Jennie, one of the most successful and gifted of all social workers, and a good friend, mother and wife, committed suicide a few weeks later. Thus, this is the real story of marijuana—a drug that will steal the very essence of being and coldly leave you in a very dark place.

Recently, a study was done in a local jail. Of some 232 inmates admitted in the course of one year, fully 93 had tested positive for marijuana upon admission. As this particular state had decriminalized marijuana, this was not arrest for simple possession but for marijuana related (caused) crime including domestic abuse and neglect, lifestyle dysfunction related crime, and other drug related crime. If some 45 percent of criminals are under the influence of marijuana at the time of the crime or arrest, and if simple possession of marijuana is not a crime they can be arrested for, then local communities and society at large need to accept that they are experiencing an epidemic of drug related crime that could be easily prevented with the proper understanding and marijuana prevention strategies.

Another woman, a functioning marijuana addict was gainfully employed and had an excellent professional career making a lot of money and "living the good life." In the beginning, like so many others, she only used it socially with friends. But she began to lose power over the drug and along with the increase in use, began isolating herself from her friends, damaging her relationships with family, and it almost led her into a nasty divorce. She lost her faith and stopped believing in God. Marijuana damaged her body, mind, relationships and soul, and lowered her moral compass into an area she thought she would never venture into. After 35 years of using marijuana she finally tried to stop but quickly realized that she couldn't. She found that she was addicted and powerless over the drug. She had to turn to professional help, and it took her three months for her system to clear of the drug effects and for her to begin to return to normal. Marijuana had become the center of her universe and nothing else was as important. She got to the point where she had to smoke it every few hours just to cope, just to be able to function at some level. This is another example where a person found out the hard way that marijuana is not a harmless or soft drug, or a drug that "hurts no one." She found out the truth, that marijuana is a seemingly subtle drug but one that leads you nowhere but which lures you into a life of lies.

One 19 year old had now quit smoking marijuana for two months. He began when he was 10 years old, and smoked "socially" until about the age of 15. Then he got a job and could afford to smoke marijuana everyday, and remained an extremely heavy smoker for the next five years smoking multiple times each day. He found that he lost interest in everything except marijuana. He was a relatively good student and participated in athletics, and thought of himself as just a casual user, but never really knew how much it was messing with his head. Looking back now, he sees how paranoid he was when he was constantly stoned. He would smoke up before and during school, and if he was around people who weren't high he would assume they were staring at him and judging his every move. It had a very negative impact on his social life, destroying it, and then he would get depressed and go on extended smoking binges that would leave him stoned for days. He didn't go a day without smoking for five years. Eventually, it had an incredibly detrimental impact on his lungs, and now he has marijuana related asthma.

This young man knows people like to downplay the effects of marijuana and say that it is relatively harmless, but the fact is that something being "relatively harmless" is still harmful. He said it is "stupid" to indulge in something that will only get you "high" for a brief period of time in exchange for so many obvious harmful side effects. He realizes now that there were much more productive things he could have been doing with his time, other than waiting for an opportunity to toke up. He also now admits that he had to take the initiative to change his life, and it was hard because he experienced marijuana withdrawal including insomnia, anxiety and decreased appetite, but says the hardest things in life are usually the most worth doing.

He used pot for almost half of his life. But now his head is clear, his memory is improving, he is more graceful in social situations without that paranoia, and he now has secured a great job. He says he is in an exciting transition and has a new lease on life. To him, it feels great not to live life revolving around a substance, and he's never been happier with himself or his life.

Another recovering marijuana addict, a man in his late twenties, used to smoke the strongest marijuana he could find, a type they called "chronic," at least an eighth of an ounce a day. He went on like this for a few years, spending at least a thousand dollars a month on cannabis, and eventually became a long term heavy user. He couldn't stop, and the very idea of not having a joint would send him into anxiety and a desperate feeling. He believes that after a few years of chronic marijuana addiction, it really started to rot his brain. His memory and cognitive ability really started to become affected. It became like he was in a constant daze, and everything around him was always cloudy. In fact, today he refers to it as marijuana induced "brain fog." He knew intuitively that cannabis was responsible for the decline in his mental state and mental health, and that it was starting to give him anxiety and depression as well. But he could not stop. He got to the point where even a small amount impaired him mentally where he struggled even with finding the right words and language and he got to a point where he could not remember even basic details. In his words he felt like a "living vegetable" as if someone had removed 90% of his brain, and was in a confused and in a constant cloud. Eventually he needed to stop driving as he was no longer safe behind the wheel.

He continue smoking even though things continued to get worse, until one night he woke up like never before—like he was in a state of shock, and "really messed up." That was the last time that he smoked marijuana.That was several years ago, and although he has made mush progress he still feels as though he has not fully recovered from the marijuana effects. He still feels in a bit of a trance, still feels like he is in a cloud of brain fog, and his intelligence, memory and cognitive abilities are significantly poorer than before he started smoking cannabis. He has no doubts that it was the marijuana that caused the serious brain damage, from which he has never properly recovered, and he still suffers from the resultant mental and emotional problems of anxiety, depression, social phobia, obsessive compulsive disorder, and has often felt suicidal.

He is yet another of the millions of former users who would say to stop using now, and that the more you smoke the worse it will get. According to this former user, brain damage is a serious thing, you only get one brain, and it can't be transplanted or easily fixed once it's damaged. He used to think marijuana was the best thing in the world and was pro-cannabis. Now he knows it is one of the most harmful and dangerous things he has ever encountered. He learned the facts the hard way.

Another young man knew some of the basics about marijuana before he ever used it including that it is psychologically addicting. He was a pretty straight teen until his junior year when he saw a lot of his classmates begin to smoke pot. He grew curious, did a little research online and through the online "experts" decided that pot posed minimal, if any, risk, so he got high. The high he experienced was intense. He thought he found "the best toy" he had ever had in his life.

For the next two years his life fluctuated trying to make up for late homework and ignored or damaged relationships. Over time, his day became more consistently "high" during which he went through several periods of wanting to commit suicide. During his last six months of use his suicidal ideation grew to the point where killing himself always seemed just a week or two away. He even formulated plans on how to do it.

Eventually his family found him stealing and gave him a choice—either treatment or jail. He chose treatment and has been clean ever since. He freely says that had he known of the devastating effects weed would have had on him, he would have never taken that first hit. He had no idea of the destructive potential of marijuana. Like so many others, when he was using he doubted he was addicted but now he sees how addicted he really was and wishes that there would be much more information made available about the addictive potential of marijuana because the "vacuum of ignorance" sucks people deeper and deeper into addiction.

One 21 year old man in the south said that, like so many others, he began smoking socially in high school, i.e., just 2 or 3 times a month. In college though, he began to smoke more heavily and then smoked for 2 years very heavily. He loved smoking so much it got to the point where he didn't even know what was going on anymore in his life. He just lived in a high haze, 24 hours per day, 7 days per week and unless he was high he felt detached—he couldn't eat, couldn't sleep, and didn't feel alive.

He finally decided to quit, only to find out that the next several weeks was a nightmare. The severity of his marijuana withdrawal symptoms was intense. He could not eat, could not sleep, experienced vivid dreams when he did nod off, and experienced body sweats, cravings, and impatience. He lost weight and spent a few days gagging uncontrollably like he was going to vomit—and sometimes did.

He realized he couldn't go back to using marijuana as it caused him so much pain in his life…neglect of his family and instead of opportunities "just stupid pipe dreams." He came to hate his marijuana addiction. Slowly he began to recover, but he experienced it as though his body went through a shock and it needed to be recalibrated.

Today he states that he can't explain the hell that he went through, and says that that's what people don't understand. Marijuana doesn't damage the body as much as causes the destruction to one's life and thoughts which in turn affects you physically and mentally and affects all those around you.

Today he says that beating the addiction is worth it. Everything is crystal clear again. He started to smoke weed to escape…but then he began living in his escape. Today he feels good again, and it's not when he is waiting before lighting up—what he feels now is real.

One female college student who had been smoking pot 3-8 times per day almost everyday, only recently realized how much she needed to quit smoking marijuana. Over the years her usage increased from once a month, to once a week, to once every day, to 3-8 times a day, every day. She didn't think she had a problem until she realized one day that the loneliness and emotional pain and emptiness and anxiety she felt was from being without marijuana, and the money she had for food and expenses all went to buy marijuana as well. She began to feel a deep guilt, but still needed to smoke.

Marijuana interfered with her college course work, her relationships, and ate away at her time that should have been spent in more positive and opportune ways. Instead, she spent her time, "stoned."

She now realizes that any boost to her ego or lift out of depression with marijuana was only a temporary fix, then it wore off until her next high. That was the circular roller coaster part of her addiction, and now she sees it actually caused her loneliness, pain, and deep introspection sometimes staring into the mirror for hours on end—sometimes seeing a beautiful, self-confident woman, sometimes seeing someone completely different and darker and with disturbed values. For this college student, when she was smoking everyday it seemed to be a battle to get through the day without feeling all those negative feelings.

She realized she had to stop and one day she did and today is clean, stronger, and doesn't ever want to touch it again.

One man bottomed out on pot when he was 26 years old. He had been using pot and alcohol since age 16, but it wasn't until he was 26 that he realized he was on a collision course with something he really didn't want—either jail, a mental institution, or a hospital.

Today he acknowledges that pot became an obstacle to his growth and his life, but it didn't start that way. When he was thirteen, he saw marijuana as an exciting diversion. It "helped him have fun", helped him forget his parents' ugly divorce and their ongoing hatred of each other.

In this situation, he readily learned pot smoking from his father. His father's daily pot-smoking had been an obstacle between them from his early childhood years. His father even got him stoned as a baby. And when he was older, he and his father experienced a "pot bond."

His smoking frequency increased from day one, so that by the time he was a freshman in college he smoked all day every day. But the marijuana took its toll and at the age of 26, he bottomed out when his problems grew and stress increased, and his paranoia and fear became intense. Instead of facing life, he had resorted to smoking pot and drinking and blocking out the unpleasantries of life.

For this man he knew his way wasn't working, so he went to a Marijuana Anonymous meeting and began working the steps. Everything in his life shifted. Today his life is busy, it is full, and it is complete. And when he has a bad day or problem, he handles it without escape into a drug. He is grateful today for everything he now has—his self-esteem, and personal integrity are restored and he no longer lives a life enslaved by marijuana.

One man who began using marijuana at age 11 had a friends who used to do heroin and crack so he thought his drug use wasn't serious, after all, "it's only weed." But eventually marijuana became the focus of his life and it took him away from the important things in life.

He began stealing and selling drugs on the streets. He got jumped and robbed often by people that used to be his friends—again, drugs turn people around (even good people.) Eventually he faced jail himself for crimes with gun charges.

Luckily, the judge let him go to a rehabilitation center instead of prison. Eventually he became comfortable, found that the people were good, and started liking and working the program and started doing things the right way. He said that they helped him realize that the way he was living life before was self-destructive and self-defeating. Now he had a chance to be productive.

Today he spends most of his time in college, working, or at home with his family, and actually likes college now, and his relationship and life have improved dramatically with his family—especially his mother. His self-esteem has improved too and now he is doing better than "most of the people who used to look down on him."

To this day he freely admits his addiction and that any dependence on marijuana is an addiction, and he says to everyone who is dependent to "get clean for yourself and for those who love you."

One young woman said when she first got high she thought it was amazing and felt great and had her "mind blown" at her new perceptions. Again, like so many others, she asked herself, "How can something so enlightening be illegal? Why have I been lied to my whole life?"

For the next four years she smoked weed almost every day. And like others, in the beginning it was fun and without any real obligations her life was pretty much care free.

Now though, she sees that almost immediately it definitely started to negatively affect her performance in all sections of her life. The quality of her work went down since she was either doing it high or just trying to finish as fast as possible so she could get high and veg out. Her social life went away since she became too self-conscious and anxious to interact with new people while high. And finally and most importantly her self-esteem and self-confidence disappeared.

Over time smoking became a habit for her. Rather than something to look forward to, it became something she needed to be able to function. The joy and enlightenment she first experienced with marijuana was long dead and replaced with anxiety filled headaches and self loathing.

Over the next few years, she tried to quit numerous times. Most were half-tried attempts lasting less than 24 hours to a week or two. But today she is clean and although isn't using, she still has headaches and "brain fog" which should clear up in time.

One long-term marijuana smoker, a smoker of over 20 years, talked about how his life had changed. He smoked pot for well over 20 years and had an endless supply of dope as he was a very resourceful and functional addict. He held down jobs, learned to invest, had relationships, had money, and looked to be a happy and stable man. But deep down inside he had an uncomfortable feeling eating away at him, his life had become unmanageable and he found that he was powerless over his pot use. He slowly, but surely, lost his confidence and his will to live life to the fullest. He became apathetic. He had gone from being a very responsible man to a lethargic non-caring one, a "life's too hard" attitude sort of person. Addiction had taken hold of him and was slowly squeezing the life out of him. He had hit a big pit in the game of life!

Now, today, two and a half years later, he is clean and sober, and a very grateful person. To quit he needed the support and help of Marijuana Anonymous. He says that he still feels a little strange as he is living without his old (supposedly) good friend, dope, but with his new ways of thinking and acting he made new and exciting friends, his old fears have diminished, and he has learned to handle new challenges. For him, life just gets better, and he is a very grateful person.

Another young adult began smoking pot when he was 18 and moved away from his family to go to college. He found that getting stoned was an instant remedy to so many of the things he didn't like about himself. He was extremely shy and smoking made him feel that he fit in. It also allowed him to be "bad," which he had never been before.

Like so many others, he dropped out of college after a couple of years because of his drug taking. Throughout his use, which continued daily for about the next twelve years, he led a life that looked functional from the outside. He always paid the rent, always had good jobs, and worked hard. Other people may have said he had an enviable life filled with variety and friends, but yet, his pot habit was something he would go to any length to hide from others. Of course, he felt guilty and ashamed of what his private life was really like.

Over the years he tried all kinds of things to stop smoking. He hated how his life became smaller and smaller. He lost confidence and isolated himself more and more. He hated how he looked and how he had to drag himself out of bed each morning. He saw his endless problems caused by marijuana—financial, physical, social, and emotional problems. His paranoia got worse and worse, and of course to deal with it he would smoke more. He realized this and began throwing his stash away every Monday morning, only to be back at the dealers that same night to get more. He finally began to take antidepressants and see therapists to deal with his depression, yet continued to use pot to cope with how lonely and bored and isolated he felt.

Finally he got desperate enough to reach out for help and went to his first Marijuana Anonymous meeting. At that meeting he found hope and support and encouragement and tools to help him quit. Three days after that meeting, he threw away his stash for the last time, and hasn't smoked since. These days he has great hope for himself and his future.

There have been millions of marijuana users and while not all became addicted or suffer consequences to a critical level, many have. Many have suffered the most painful of circumstances because of this "benign" drug, and have lost quality in life and or potential years of life. Their stories are testimonies to the truth and realities about marijuana. Marijuana is a powerful, toxic, and mind-altering addictive psychoactive drug. The key is to learn about it, become self-aware, to understand what it really is—a drug, and above all to resolve not to use it or to quit before it enslaves you.

# FINAL THOUGHTS

*There are more people in the U.S. addicted to marijuana than to prescription drugs, and once it is legalized and commercialized the marijuana use rates will skyrocket comparable to those of alcohol or tobacco.*

The premise of this book is that marijuana is a powerful, toxic and addictive psychoactive drug. Every year there are hundreds-of-thousands of marijuana related admissions into hospital emergency rooms. Every year there are hundreds-of-thousands of admissions into treatment centers where marijuana is either a primary or secondary drug of addiction. Every year there are thousands of admissions into mental health clinics because of marijuana exacerbated mental illness. Every year there are thousands of injuries and accident fatalities because of the growing incidence of driving while under the influence of marijuana. Every year there are thousands of people sentenced to jail for crimes related to marijuana use. Every year thousands find that marijuana negatively affected their academic performance, or find themselves on welfare, in family court, or homeless or jobless because of the long term effects of marijuana. The premise of this book is well supported and well documented by research. Marijuana is a dangerous drug, and the consumption of marijuana is not recommended.

Furthermore, research paints a grim picture for marijuana users who start at a young age:

— Teens using marijuana before age 18 are two-to-four times more likely to develop psychosis as young adults compared to those who do not.

— The teen brain is much more vulnerable to addiction. Of those who try marijuana before age 18, 1-in-6 youth will either abuse it or become addicted to it, compared with 1-in-25 adults.

— Studies show that heavy doses of THC change the way the brain develops and especially affects the hippocampus which is critical for learning and memory, and adolescents who start using marijuana between the ages of 14 and 22 (and stop by 22) still have many more cognitive deficits at age 27 than non-using peers.

— The more often teens use and the greater the dose, the more reckless their behavior becomes, so regular marijuana use puts them at greater risk for dropping out of school, engaging in risky sex behaviors, and getting in accidents—the leading cause of death for adolescents.

An undercover officer with a drug task force said he is seeing more and younger teens bringing marijuana to schools, in sometimes-surprising quantities. "When we have middle school kids show up with a half an ounce, that is shocking to me," he said.

A program manager for at-risk students said, "We have seen a sharp rise in drug-related disciplinary actions which… is being attributed to the changing social norms surrounding marijuana." She said school officials believe the jump is linked to the message that legalization is sending to youth: that marijuana is a medicine and is a safe and accepted recreational activity. She also believes that greater availability is a factor.

A clinic counselor said he is very upset with the "pervasive use" of marijuana throughout the city—including at parks, public places, hotels and even office buildings. He said he felt "violated" and could not wait to leave (those areas.) He said, "Legalization will be reversed in only a matter of a few years…It's out of control."

Joseph Califano, former Secretary of Health, Education and Welfare, and President of the National Center on Addiction and Substance Abuse at Columbia University has written numerous articles on the dangers of marijuana. Patrick Kennedy, former Congressman and a spokesperson for Project SAM (Smart Approaches to Marijuana) is opposed to the legalization of marijuana. Former Drug Enforcement Agency administrator Peter Bensinger who said the rapid growth and acceptance of marijuana is a disaster and will damage the young people (in those states), is opposed to the legalization of marijuana. Dr. Nora Volkow, the director of the National Institute on Drug Abuse, states that "marijuana is not safe." Dr. Christian Thurston, a treatment specialist is totally opposed to marijuana—one of his findings is that while adolescents have always been impulsive thrill seekers "all the most dangerous behaviors escalate when teens use marijuana."

In terms of adult use, Conspire, a company in Colorado that provides drug testing to businesses and schools, has found that the number of their clientele testing positive for THC has risen 44% from December, 2013 (a 270% increase since legalization began in 2009.) Ben Cort, from the Center for Dependency, Addiction, and Rehabilitation at the University of Colorado Hospital, stated, "Given the significant change in attitudes in Colorado towards marijuana, and the increased number of people using the drug and adolescents seeking treatment for it, I am not surprised by these numbers. As the adults and children of Colorado continue to be inundated by marijuana marketing, I expect to see these numbers to increase even more—resulting in millions of dollars in social costs."

Experts are also concerned about a newly emerging trend, parents who smoke marijuana either when their children know it, smoke in front of their children, or even with their children. Forest Tennent, M.D., an adolescent specialist once said, "Parents: if you are a non-smoking, non-drinking, churchgoing, consistent, family-oriented, loving, disciplinarian, the odds are overwhelmingly in your favor that you will raise a positive, drug-free child." His primary concern was that the behavior of parents is a strong influence—if not the determining factor, in shaping the behavior of youth.

In the case of marijuana use, children are found to more likely use marijuana if their parents did. A government study by the Department of Health and Human Services of 9,463 parents and children found that children whose parents used marijuana are more likely to use the drug as well. The study found that parents who used marijuana multiple times and who do not view the drug as risky were more likely to have children who felt the same way. "The study points out, once again, the power of parents to help their children stay healthy and drug-free," said the Substance Abuse and Mental Health Services Administration. "It found that parents' attitudes and drug-use history had an effect on their children's likelihood of marijuana and other drug use." This dynamic also reflects what treatment providers so often see: children who have parents who smoke, drink, or use drugs or who speak with profanity, usually copy their parent's values, attitudes and behaviors. Children are a microcosm of their family and environment.

Marijuana has increased in potency since the 1970s. Higher THC content can contribute to psychotic and other reactions (anxiety, agitation, delusions, amnesia, confusion, and hallucinations), increase the users' risk of developing dependence on the drug, and increase the risk of personal, family and social problems. New research now links marijuana use to fetal drug affects, cancer, the amotivation syndrome, mood changes, depression, fatigue, memory problems, hypersensitivity to criticism, underachievement, confusion or mental impairment, deteriorating academic performance, outbursts of anger, panic attacks, hostility with lack of insight/remorse, driving while impaired, accidents, tolerance, dependency, physical addiction, and a host of other problems.

There have been hundreds of articles and studies released demonstrating the true negative consequences from both incidental and heavy marijuana use, again, as a major detriment to the quality of life that society wants to establish and guide in the United States.

*After reviewing—literally—hundreds of articles and studies on marijuana, this author has never seen even one study that even hints that marijuana is a protective factor or good for positive youth development, that marijuana use supports healthy families, or that concludes that marijuana use builds strong communities. In fact, in study after study, overwhelmingly, the findings are exactly the opposite for all three cases.*

Marijuana use will definitely increase if it's legalized. Accessibility and availability are prime determinants in the level of drug use. As marijuana use increased with decriminalization and then again with the legalization of medical marijuana, experts acknowledge that it will most certainly increase even more dramatically with full legalization. Perhaps the worse defense for the legalization of marijuana is the comparison with alcohol and tobacco which are legal, the fact is that this is exactly why marijuana should not be legalized. With greater accessibility and availability there will be greater use, and consequently, more abuse, more dependency, and more individual, family and social problems as a simple outcome.

It is also predicted that research will soon better define three other negative consequences of marijuana use: the pronounced negative effects on relationships—especially long term, intimate relationships; the effects on personality development; and soon research will begin to more clearly define the effects not just on youth but on adults as well.

As a final thought, reflect upon the hype and propaganda of the legalization movement. There is a great deal of literature available which is "pro-marijuana" literature, and the vast majority of the hundreds of marijuana internet sites are pro-marijuana sites. One should not be mislead by all the pro-marijuana literature that is available, however. A review of that literature suggests that much of it is written from a biased point of view and is suspect, misleading, or dismisses accurate findings by confusing or negating important factors. Much of it is reprocessed from old reports and studies which are no longer valid. In addition, much is based upon misinterpretation of the facts, and based on simple opinion rather than fact.

The American Medical Association, the American Psychiatric Association, National Families in Action, the American Society of Addiction Medicine, Churches across the country, prevention and treatment specialists, schools, PTA/PTO groups, law enforcement organizations, health organizations, etc., virtually every organization that cares about the health, safety and welfare of youth and families, is opposed to the further legalization of marijuana.

According to one renowned clinical researcher, even if an article does disprove a certain reported negative consequence of marijuana, it can never prove that marijuana in any way or manner is a safe drug. There is just too much evidence to the contrary.

Of course, not everyone who smokes marijuana will suffer serious negative consequences. The consequences of drug use are related to the frequency and pattern of use, the nature of the drug, the potency of the drug, and the set and setting of use. Perhaps more importantly, however, it is also directly related to individual risk factors, and these are often idiosyncratic and usually underestimated until it is too late and the drug has done its damage.

Here then, lies one of the greatest dangers of marijuana: *it is underestimated as a powerful pharmacologic, mind-altering substance.* In this regard, it is not fully appreciated for what it really is—people do not give it serious consideration. Society disregards the inherent dangers, and before they know it at least 10-to-25 percent of users (up to 75 percent of teens) experience marijuana related problems, many of which are grave and even catastrophic consequences. If then, as according to some exerts, 10-25 percent of marijuana users will experience harmful effects even to the point of ruin, does that not qualify marijuana as a toxic substance?

As a final consideration, reflect upon the overall premise of this book. If what this author is saying is wrong and marijuana remains illegal and is not legalized, then there is no harm done…yes, people will be denied greater accessibility to the drug marijuana or people will not be making as much money from the marijuana industry but the actual harm is minimal. If what this author is saying is true, however, and marijuana is still legalized despite these dangers then hundreds of thousands of people will be harmed and hundreds of thousands of families will suffer the (sometimes) devastating consequences of use and dependency.

Everyone wants a happy and healthy life. Many have found, though, that the quality of life they wanted and expected never materialized, that their dreams turned into nightmares, that their potential in life was lost, and that their hopes slowly faded away, simply because a friend said *"Try this, it won't hurt you."* But listen to recovering addicts, the real experts, and you will hear many say, *"That stuff messed me up and burned me out!"*

Marijuana use is contra-indicated for a healthy life. Many tens-of-thousands will attest that it really is a Weapon of Mass Destruction!

# REFERENCES

"Adverse Health Effects of Marijuana Use," Nora D. Volkow, M.D., Ruben D. Baler, Ph.D., Wilson M. Compton, M.D., and Susan R.B. Weiss, Ph.D., New England Journal of Medicine, June 2014.

"Drug Harms in the UK: A Multicriteria Decision Analysis", Professors David J. Nutt, FMedSci, Leslie A. King, PhD, and Lawrence D. Phillips, PhD. on behalf of the Independent Scientific Committee on Drugs.

"Early Findings in Controlled Studies of Herbal Cannabis: A Review", Andrea Barthwell, M.D., FASAM, Journal of Global Drug Policy and Practice, June 24, 2010.

"The Economic Impacts of Marijuana Legalization", David G. Evans, Esq., The Journal of Global Drug Policy and Practice, Volume 7, Issue 4, Winter 2013.

"The Legalization of Marijuana in Colorado: The Impact", (Volume 1), Rocky Mountain High Intensity Drug Trafficking Area (RMHIDTA), August 2013.

"Diffusion Abnormalities in Adolescents and Young Adults with a History of Heavy Cannabis Use", Ashtari, M., Cervellione, K., Cottone, J., Ardekani, B.A., Kumra, S., Journal of Psychiatric Research, January 2009.

U.S. Department of Justice, "DEA Position on Marijuana," Drug Enforcement Administration (DEA), Washington, DC U.S.A. July 2010.

"Heavy Marijuana Users Have Abnormal Brain Structure and Poor Memory", Matthew Smith, John Csernansky, M.D., Hans Breiter, M.D., Northwestern University Feinberg School of Medicine, Schizophrenia Bulletin, December 2013.

Brady, J.E. and Li, G., "Trends in Alcohol and Other Drugs Detected in Fatally Injured Drivers in the United States, 199-2010," American Journal of Epidemiology, 1/29/2014.

Speaking Out Against Drug Legalization, Drug Enforcement Administration.

"Non-medical Marijuana: Rite of Passage or Russian Roulette?" The National Center on Addiction at Columbia University, July 1999.

"Escalation of Marijuana Use: Application of a General Theory of Deviant Behavior", Kaplan, H.B., Martin, S.S., Johnson, R.J., and Robbins, C.A., Journal of Health and Social Behavior, 1986.

Clayton, R.R., and Leukefeld, C.G., "The Prevention of Drug Use Among Youth; Implications of Legalization", Journal of Primary Prevention, 1992.

Rosalie Liccardo Pacula, "Marijuana Use and Policy: What We Know and Have Yet to Learn", NBER Reporter: Research Summary (2005).

R. L. Pacula and B. Kilmer, "Marijuana and Crime: Is there a Connection beyond Prohibition?" NBER Working Paper No. 10046, October 2003.

National Drug Intelligence Center, Domestic Cannabis Cultivation Assessment (2007.)

American Psychiatric Association. Diagnostic and Statistical Manual of Mental Disorders Fifth Edition DSM-5, American Psychiatric Association. 2013.

Justice Institute of British Columbia. Substance Use/Misuse Certificate Program. Victoria, BC. 2001.

"Cannabis Withdrawal in the United States: Results from NESARC," Hasin DS, Journal Clinical Psychiatry, September 2008.

"Psychiatric Symptoms in Male Cannabis Users not using other Illicit Drugs", Troisi, Pasini, Saacco, Spalletta, Addiction, April 1998.

"Cannabis Use Correlates with Schizotypy in Healthy People", Williams, Wellman, Rawlins, Addiction, June 1996.

"The Human Toxicity Of Marijuana", Nahas, Latour, Medical Journal of Australia, April 1992.

"Marijuana Use, Introspectiveness, and Mental Health", Zablocki, Aidala, Hansell, White; Journal of Health and Social Behavior, March 1991.

"Marijuana: Medical Implications" (American Family Physician, December 1999), John Hubbard, M.D., PhD., Sharone E. Franco, M.D., and Emmanuel S. Onaivi, PhD.

"Alcohol Use, Illicit Drug Use and Road Rage", Fierro I., Journal of Studies on Alcohol and Drugs, March 2011.

"Explaining Associations Between Cannabis Use Disorders in Adolescence and Later Major Depression: A Test of the Psychosocial Failure Model", Naomi R. Marmorstein, Ph.D., and William G. Iacono, Ph.D.

"Substance-Dependent, Conduct-Disordered Adolescent Males: Severity of Diagnosis Predicts 2-Year Outcome", Crowley, Miikulich, MacDonald, Young, Zerbe, Journal of Drug and Alcohol Dependence, February 1, 1998.

"Treated Delinquent Boys Substance Use: Onset, Pattern, Relationship to Conduct and Mood Disorders", Young, Mikulich, Goodwin, Hardy, Martin, Zoccolillo, Crowley, Journal of Drug and Alcohol Dependence, February 1995.

"Correlates of Depression in Primary Care", Rowe, Fleming, Barry, Manwell, Kropp, Journal of Family Practice, December 8, 1995.

"The Association of Anti-social Personality Symptoms with Marijuana Abuse/Dependence. A Monozygotic Co-Twin Study", Scherrer, Lin,Eisen, Goldberg, True, Lyons, Tsuang; Journal of Nervous and Mental Disorders; October 1996.

"Anti-Social Behavior: Its Relation to Selected Sociodemographic Variables and Alcohol and Drug Use Among Mexican Students", Substance Use and Misuse, 1998.

Diagnostic and Statistical Manual of Mental Disorders, 4th Edition, American Psychiatric Association, 1994.

"Cannabinoids and Psychosis", Sewell, R.A., Ranganathan, M., & D'Souza, D.C., International Review of Psychiatry, (2009.)

"Substance Use in Adolescence and Psychosis: Clarifying the Relationship", Barkus, E., & Murray, R. M., Annual Review of Clinical Psychology, 2010.

Cannabis-induced Mania? A Case Study and Literature Review, Matthijs, N., Touquet, G., & De Hert, MTijdschrift Voor Psychiatrie, 2009.

Testing Hypotheses About the Relationship Between Cannabis Use and Psychosis, Degenhardt, L., Hall, W., & Lynskey, M., Drug and Alcohol Dependence, 2003.

Drug Abuse and Aggression Between Intimate Partners: A Meta-Analytic Review. Moore, T.M., Stuart, G.L., Meehan, J.C., Rhatigan, D.L., Hellmuth, J.C., & Keen, S.M., Clinical Psychology Review, 2008.

"Change Your Brain, Change Your Life", Daniel G. Amen, M.D., professor of psychiatry and human behavior at the University of California, Director of the Amen Clinics.

"Early Adolescent Marijuana Use: Risks for The Transition to Young Adulthood", Brook, J.S., Adams, R.E., Balka, E.B., and Johnson, E., Psychological Medicine, 2002.

"Stress-Related Factors in Cannabis Use and Misuse: Implications for Prevention and Treatment", Scott M. Hyman, Ph.D. and Rajita Sinha, Ph.D., Yale University School of Medicine, Department of Psychiatry, Journal of Substance Abuse Treatment, June 2009.

"Neuroimaging Marijuana Use and its Effects on Cognitive Function", Krista Lisdahl Medina and Susan Tapert, presented at the annual meeting of the American Academy of Pediatrics in Boston, Massachusetts, 2008.

Cannabis Use and Later Life Outcomes, Fergusson, D. M., & Boden, J. M., Addiction, 2008.

"Cannabis Use and Mental Health in Young People: Cohort Study." British Medical Journal, Patton, GC, 2002.

World Health Organization Project on Health Implications of Cannabis Use, 1999.

The Influence of Marijuana Use on Neurocognitive Functioning in Adolescents, Schweinsburg, A.D.; Brown, S.A.; and Tapert, S.F., Curr Drug Abuse Rev, 2008

Psychological and Social Sequelae of Cannabis and other Illicit Drug Use by Young People, Macleod, J.; Oakes, R.; Copello, A.; Crome, I.; Egger, M.; Hickman, M.;

Oppenkowski, T.; Stokes-Lampard, H.; and Davey Smith, G., Lancet 2004.

Drug Abuse and Aggression Between Intimate Partners, Moore, T.M., Stuart, G.L., Meehan, J.C., Rhatigan, D.L., Hellmuth, J.C., & Keen, S.M., Clinical Psychology Review, 2008.

Drugs and Driving by American High School Seniors, O'Malley, P.M., and Johnston, L.D., Journal Studies Alcohol Drugs, 2007.

Drugs of Abuse, Driving and Traffic Safety, Penning, R., Veldstra, J. L., Daamen, A. P., Olivier, B., & Verster, J. C., Current Drug Abuse Reviews, 2010.

Dose Related Risk of Motor Vehicle Crashes After Cannabis Use, Ramaekers, J. G., Berghaus, G., van Laar, M., & Drummer, O. H., Drug and Alcohol Dependence, 2004.

"New Study Reveals Scope of Drug and Crime Connection", May 28, 2009, National Office of Drug Control Policy.

"Behind Bars II: Substance Abuse and America's Prison Population", CASA at Columbia University, February 2010.

"Marijuana And Crime: Is There A Connection Beyond Prohibition?", R.L. Pacula, B. Kilmer, National Bureau Of Economic Research, October 2003.

Acute Cardiovascular Fatalities Following Cannabis Use, Bachs, L., & Mørland, H., Forensic Science International, 2001.

Cannabis Smoking and Risk of Lung Cancer in Men: a Pooled Analysis, Berthiller, J., Straif, K., Boniol, M., Voirin, N., Benhaïm-Luzon, V., Ayoub, W. B., Dari, I., Journal of Thoracic Oncology, 2008.

Impairment Due to Cannabis and Ethanol: Clinical Signs and Additive Effects, Bramness, J. G., Khiabani, H. Z., & Mørland, J., Addiction, 2010.

Association of Marijuana Use and the Incidence of Testicular Germ Cell Tumors, Daling, J. R., Doody, D. R., Sun, X., Trabert, B. L., Weiss, N. S., Chen, C., Biggs, M. L., Cancer, 2009.

Adverse Effects of Cannabis, Hall, W. & Solowij, N., Lancet, 1998.

"Development and Consequences of Cannabis Dependence", Budney, A. J., & Moore, B. A Journal of Clinical Pharmacology, 2002.

National Institute on Drug Abuse—2005, Marijuana Abuse (NIDA Research Report Series No. 05-3859), Bethesda, MD.

"Marijuana—Medical Implications", American Family Physician, December 1999.

Epidemiologic Review of Marijuana Use and Cancer Risk, Hashibe, M., Straif, K., Tashkin, D. P., Morgenstern, H., Greenland, S., & Zhang, Z., Alcohol, 2005.

Role of Cannabinoids in the Development of Fatty Liver, Purohit, V., Rapaka, R., & Shurtleff, D., The AAPS Journal, 2010.

"Chronic Toxicology of Cannabis", Clinical Toxicology. Reece, A.S., (2009).

"Cannabinoid Hyperemesis", Canadian Journal of Gastroenterology, Sullivan S. (2010).

"Identifying Prenatal Cannabis Exposure And Effects Of Concurrent Tobacco Exposure On Neonatal Growth", Gray, TR, Eiden, RD, Leonard, KE, Shisler, S, Huestis, MA; Chemistry and Drug Metabolism, Intramural Research Program, National Institute on Drug Abuse, Clinical Chemistry, September 2010.

"Developmental Consequences Of Perinatal Cannabis Exposure: Behavioral And Neuroendocrine Effects In Adult Rodents", Campolongo P, Trezza V, Ratano P, Cuoo V; Department of Physiology and Pharmacology, Sapienza University of Rome; Psychopharmacology (Berl) June 2010.

"Adolescent Self-Reported Behaviors and Their Association with Marijuana Use", Janet C. Greenblatt, June 03, 2008, Source: Office of Applied Studies, SAMHSA, National Household Survey on Drug Abuse.

"Marijuana—Medical Implications", John R. Hubbard, M.D., Ph.D., Sharonee E. Franco, M.D., and Emmanuel S. Onaivi, Ph.D., Vanderbilt University School of Medicine, Nashville, Tennessee, American Family Physician, December 1999.

"Prenatal Marijuana and Nicotine Exposure Linked to Teen Neurologic Deficits", American Academy of Child and Adolescent Psychiatry 54th Annual Meeting: Symposium, October 31, 2007 (Medscape Medical News, 2007).

"Cannabis Chemical Harms Embryo", Proceedings of the National Academy of Sciences, Vanderbilt University Medical Centre, BBC News, November 2003.

"Developmental Exposure to Cannabinoids Causes Subtle and Enduring Neurofunctional Alterations", Campolongo, P., Trezza, V., Palmery, M., Trabace, L., & Cuomo, V. International Review of Neurobiology, 2009.

"Adverse Effects Of Cannabis On Health: An Update Of The Literature Since 1996", Kalant, H., Progress in Neuro-Psychopharmacology and Biological Psychiatry, 2004.

"Marijuana—Medical Implications", American Family Physician, Hubbard, Franco, and Onaivi, December 1999.

"Long-Term Cannabis Use: Characteristics of Users in an Australian Rural Area", Reilly D., Didcott P, Swift W. Hall W., Northern Rivers Health Service, Lismore, New South Wales, Australia, June 1998.

"Marijuana and Anti-depressants Don't Mix", Dr. Istvan Boksay, Spotlight Health, January 24,2001.

"I'll Quit Tomorrow", Vernon E. Johnson, HarperSanFrancisco, 1990.

"Cannabis: Effects of Consumption on Health", by INSERM (Institut National de la Santé et de la Recherche Médicale; French Institute of Health and Medical Research, 2001.

Chronic Toxicology of Cannabis, Reece, A.S., Clinical Toxicology (2009).

"High Resolution Brain SPECT Imaging—Marijuana Smokers with AD/HD", Daniel Amen, M.D., Journal of Psychoactive Drugs, Volume 30, No. 2, April-June 1998.

"Corpus Callosum Damage in Heavy Marijuana use: Preliminary Evidence from Diffusion Tensor Tractography and Tract-Based Spatial Statistics", Arnone, D., T.R. Barrick, S. Chengappa, C.E. Mackay, C.A. Clark, and M.T. Abou-Saleh, 2008,

"Regional Brain Abnormalities Associated with Heavy Long-Term Cannabis Use", Yücel, M., N. Solowij, C. Respondek, S. Whittle, A. Fornito, C. Pantelis, and D.I. Lubman, Archives of General Psychiatry, 2008.

"Changes in Brain Function During Acute Cannabis Intoxication: Preliminary Findings Suggest a Mechanism for Cannabis-Induced Violence, Criminal Behavior and

Mental Health," Howard, R.C. and D.B. Menkes, Brief Report, 2007.

Licit and Illicit Drugs; The Consumers Union Report on Narcotics, Stimulants, Depressants, Inhalants, Hallucinogens, and Marijuana; Edward M. Brecher, October 1, 1973.

"Marijuana Use is Associated With a Reorganized Visual-Attention Network and Cerebellar Hypoactivation Brain," Chang, L., R. Yakupov, C. Cloak and T. Ernst, 2006.

"Drug Use and the Risk of Major Depressive Disorder, Alcohol Dependence, and Substance Use Disorders," Brook, D., Brook, J., Zhang, C., Cohen P., & Whiteman, M., Archives of General Psychiatry, 2002.

Marijuana Use is Associated with Impaired Sleep Quality; Dr. Michael Grandner, Jilesh Chheda, American Academy of Sleep Medicine, June 2014.

Cannabis Use Is Quantitatively Associated with Nucleus Accumbens and Amygdala Abnormalities in Young Adult Recreational Users; Jodi M. Gilman, John K. Kuster, Sang Lee, Myung Joo Lee, Byoung Woo Kim, Nikos Makris, Andre van der Kouwe, Anne J. Blood, and Hans C. Breiter, Journal of Neuroscience, March 2014.

Adverse Effects of Marijuana Use; Nora D. Volkow, M.D., Ruben D. Baler, Ph.D., Wilson M. Compton, M.D., and Susan R.B. Weiss, Ph.D., New England Journal of Medicine, June 2014.

The Cannabis Withdrawal Syndrome, Budney AJ, Hughes JR., Current Opinion Psychiatry, 2006.

Opposite Effects of Delta-9-tetrahydrocannabinol and Cannabidiol on Human Brain Function and Psychopathology, Bhattacharyya S, Morrison PD, Fusar-Poli P, et al. Neuropsychopharmacology, 2010.

Physicians and Medical Marijuana, Kleber HD, DuPont RL, American Journal of Psychiatry, 2012.

Marijuana use and Risk of Lung Cancer: a 40-year cohort study, Callaghan RC, Allebeck P, Sidorchuk A., Cancer Causes Control, 2013.

Persistent Cannabis Users Show Neuropsychological Decline from Childhood to Midlife, Meier MH, Caspi A, Ambler A., Proc National Academy of Science, 2012.

Cannabis Use and Risk of Psychotic or Affective Mental Health Outcomes: A Systematic Review, Moore TH, Zammit S, Lingford-Hughes A., Lancet, 2007.

# RESOURCES

Addiction Research Foundation
Amen Clinics
American Journal of Psychiatry
American Medical Association
American Psychiatric Association
American Psychological Association
Archives of General Psychiatry
Archives of Sexual Behavior
British Journal of Psychiatry
Canadian Centre on Substance Abuse (CCSA)
Center for Substance Abuse Research
Center on Young Adult Health and Development, University of Maryland
Community Anti-Drug Coalitions of America (CADCA)
Department of Health and Human Services TEDS (Treatment Episode Data Set)
Drug Abuse Warning Network (DAWN)
Federal Bureau of Investigation
International Medical Journal Lancet
Join Together
Journal of Addictive Behaviors
Journal of the American Academy of Child and Adolescent Psychiatry
Journal of the Canadian Medical Association
Journal of Neuropsychopharmacology
Journal of Psychiatric Research
Journal of Psychoactive Drugs
Journal of Sexual Medicine
Journal of Studies on Alcohol and Drugs
National Academy of Science Institute of Medicine

National Cannabis Prevention and Information Centre in Australia
National Center on Addiction and Substance Abuse at Columbia University
National Council on Alcoholism and Drug Dependence (NCADD)
National Drug Intelligence Center
National Epidemiologic Survey on Alcohol and Related Conditions
National Families in Action (NFIA)
National Institute of Justice Arrestee Drug Abuse Monitoring (ADAM) Program
National Highway Traffic Safety Administration Fatality Analysis Reporting System
National Institute on Drug Abuse, Research Report Series Marijuana Abuse
National Research Council
National Survey on Drug Use and Health (NSDUH)
Office of National Drug Control Policy
Proceedings of the National Academy of Sciences
Queensland Brain Institute and School of Population Health
School of Public Health, Columbia University
Smart Approaches to Marijuana
United Nations World Drug Report
University of Washington Alcohol and Drug Abuse Institute
WebMD
Youth Justice Board, United Kingdom

# MARIJUANA REFERRAL RESOURCES

*A life is a terrible thing to waste!*

If you have a problem with marijuana,
if you feel as if you are losing control of your life…
reach out to a local alcohol/drug treatment agency
or call or attend a meeting of
Marijuana Anonymous
or
Narcotics Anonymous.

They are friends who understand
and will help you to break free from the bonds of compulsion
and find a new serenity and a new peace.

It may just save a life.